The Confluence American Aut Y0-DUD-482

James R. Hepworth, Series

Lewis-Clark State College

James Welch

TCAAS 1

ERRATA

Preface

P. viii. line 5. *"Sand's"* should read *"Sands'."*
P. xiv. line 11. *"revised edition published."* should read
  "(revised edition) published."
P. 10. line 8. Delete entire line.
P. 30. line 28. *"machanics"* should read *"mechanics."*
P. 30. line 35. *"Objiway"* should read *"Ojibway."*
P. 31. line 12. *"assimulate"* should read *"assimilate."*
P. 39. line 25. *"Blackfoot"* should read *"Blackfeet."*
P. 39. line 26. *"unccountably"* should read
  "unaccountably."
P. 40. line 28. *"Blackfoot"* should read *"Blackfeet."*
P. 49. line 27. *"anti-climatic"* should read
  "anti-climactic."
P. 55. line 7. *"("* should read *"[."*
P. 55. line 8. *")"* should read *"]."*
P.106. line 13. *"origianl"* should read *"original."*
P.106. line 23. *"Le'vi-"* should read *"Levi-."*
P.116. line 25. *"bones.".* should read *"bones."*
P.132. line 30. *"assoiciated"* should read *"associated."*
P.147. line 12. *"emascualted"* should read *"emasculated."*
P.149. line 4. *"barwoman"* should read *"bar woman."*
P.149. line 31. *"he more"* should read *"he is more."*
P.150. line 16. *"liason"* should read *"liaison."*
P.151. line 37. *"throught"* should read *"through."*
P.152. line 3. *"Washinton"* should read *"Washington."*
P.153. line 27. *"completetly"* should read
  "completely."
P.156. line 19. *"anouncement"* should read
  "announcement."
P.157. line 1. *"offered Rhea"* should read *"offered by
  Rhea."*
P.168. line 32. *"his tail"* should read *"his-tail."*
P.169. line 20. *"tast"* should read *"taste."*

1

The following items were inadvertently excluded from Ron McFarland's, "James Welch: A Bibliography." These items should constitute the bottom line on page 191 and following.

___ and A. LaVonne Ruoff, eds. "A Discussion of *Winter in the Blood.*" *American Indian Quarterly,* 4 (May 1978), 159-68.

Espey, David B. "Endings in Contemporary American Indian Fiction." *Western American Literature,* 13 (August 1978), 133-39.

Horton, Andrea. "The Bitter Humor of *Winter in the Blood.*" *American Indian Quarterly,* 4 (May 1978), 131-39.

Jahner, Elaine. "Quick Paces and a Space of Mind." *The University of Denver Quarterly,* 14 *(Winter 1980). 34-47.*

___ "A Critical Approach to American Indian Literature." *In Studies in American Indian Literature.* Paula Gunn Allen ed. New York: MLA, 1983. Pp. 220-223.

Kunz, Don. "Lost in the Distance of Winter: James Welch's *Winter in the Blood.*" *Critique: Studies in Modern Fiction,* 20 (August 1978), 93-99.

Larson, Charles R. *American Indian Fiction.* Albuquerque: University of New Mexico Press, 1978. Pp. 133-154.

Larson, Sidner. "James Welch's *Winter in the Blood.*" *Indian Historian,* 10 (Winter 1977), 23-26.

Lincoln, Kenneth. *Native American Renaissance.* Berkeley: University of California Press, 1983.

___ "Back-Tracking James Welch." *Multi-Ethnic Literatures of the United States* (MELUS), 6 (Spring 1979), 23-40.

Milton, John R. "New American Indian Writers." In *The Contemporary Literary Scene,* 1973. Frank N. Magill, ed. Englewood Cliffs, New Jersey: Salem Press, 1974. Pp. 82-86.

Rhodes, Geri. *"Winter in the Blood*—Bad Medicine in the Blood." *New American,* 2 (Summer/Fall 1976), 44-49.

Ruoff A. LaVonne. "Alienation and the Female Principle in *Winter in the Blood.*" *American Indian Quarterly* 4 (May 1978), 107-22. Reprinted herein.

___"History in *Winter in the Blood:* Backgrounds and Bibliography." *American Indian Quarterly,* 4 (May 1978),169-72.

Sands, Kathleen M. "Alienation and Broken Narrative in Winter in the Blood." *American Indian Quarterly,* 4 (May 1978), 97-105.

Smith, William F., Jr. *"Winter in the Blood:* The Indian Cowboy as Everyman." *Michigan Academician,* 10 (Winter 1978). 299-306.

Thackeray, William W. " 'Crying for Pity' in *Winter in the Blood." MELUS,* 7 (Spring 1980). 61-78.

Velie, Alan R. *"Winter in the Blood* as Comic Novel." *American Indian Quarterly,* 4 (May 1978), 141-47.

___"Winter in the Blood:* Welch and the Comic Novel." In *Four American Indian Literary Masters.* Norman: University of Oklahoma Press, 1982. Pp. 91-103.

Von Freydorf, Roswith. "James Welch, eine junge Stimme Alt-Amerikas." In *Geschichte und Gesellschaft in der amerikanischen Literatur.* Karl Schubert and Ursula Muller-Richter, eds. Heidelberg: Quelle and Meyer, 1975. Pp. 252-281.

THE DEATH OF JIM LONEY

Selected Reviews and Essays

Broyard, Anatole. Review. *New York Times,* 129 (November 28, 1979), C-25.

Carr, Helen. Review. *Times Literary Supplement,* -4023 (May 2, 1980), 500.

Crace, Jim. Review. *New Statesman,* 99 (May 2, 1980), 682.

Hoxie, Frederick E. Review. *Antioch Review,* 38 (Summer 1989).386-387.

Kiely, Robert. Review. *New York Times Book Review* (November 4, 1979), 14.

Lewis, Robert W. Review. *Studies in American Literature* 4 (Summer 1980). 179-186.

___ "James Welch's *The Death of Jim Loney." Studies*

in *American Indian Literature*, 5 (Fall 1981), 3-5.

Logan, William. Review. *Saturday Review*, 6 (November 10, 1979), 54.

Pavich, Paul. Review. *Western American Literature*, 15 (Fall, 1980), 219-220.

Sands, Kathleen M. *"The Death of Jim Loney:* Indian or Not?" *Studies in American Literature*, 5 (Fall 1981), 5-8. Reprinted in this volume.

Schneider, Jack W. "The New Indian: Alienation and the Rise of the Indian Novel." *South Dakota Review*, 17 (Winter 1979-1980), 67-76.

Thackeray, William W. *"The Death of Jim Loney* as a Half-Breed's Tragedy." *Studies in American Literature*, 5 (Fall 1981), 2-3.

Turner, Frederick. Review. *Nation*, 229 (November 24, 1979), 538-539.

Wanner, Irene. Review. *Iowa Review*, 10 (Fall 1979), 110-111.

Woodard, Charles. Review. *World Literature Today*, 54 (Summer 1980), 437-474.

Other Reviews

Atlantic, 244 (October 1979), 108; *Best Sellers*, 39 (December 1979), 327; *Booklist*, 76 (October 15, 1979), 334; *Kirkus*, 47 (July 1, 1979), 762 and (July 15, 1979), 802;*Library Journal*, 104 (September 1, 1979), 1722; *Observer* (April 27, 1980), 39; *Publishers' Weekly*, 216 (July 23, 1979), 155; *Studies in American Indian Literature*, 5 (Fall 1981), 1.

The Confluence American Authors Series

James Welch

Edited by

Ron McFarland

Confluence Press, Inc.   Lewiston, Idaho

Acknowledgements

All excerpts for the texts of James Welch's writing are reprinted by permission of the author and publisher. Permission to reproduce the James Welch writings in this volume must be obtained from them.

From *Winter in the Blood* by James Welch. Copyright © 1974 by James Welch. Reprinted and excerpted by permission of James Welch and Harper and Row.

"Magic Fox," "The World's Only Corn Palace," "Riding the Earthboy 40," "There Is A Right Way." "Grandma's Man," "Going to Remake This World," "The Only Bar in Dixon," "Surviving," "Gravely," and "Grandfather at the Rest Home" from *Riding the Earthboy 40* by James Welch. Copyright © 1976 by James Welch. Reprinted and excerpted by permission of Harper and Row. Revised Edition.

From *The Death of Jim Loney* by James Welch. Copyright © 1979 by James Welch. Reprinted and excerpted by permission of James Welch and Harper and Row.

From *Untitled Novel in Progress* by James Welch. Copyright © 1986 by James Welch. Reprinted and excerpted by permission of James Welch.

"Alienation and the Female Principle in *Winter in the Blood*" by A. LaVonne Ruoff. Copyright © 1978 by A. LaVonne Ruoff. Revised and reprinted by permission of A. LaVonne Ruoff. Copyright © 1986 by A. LaVonne Ruoff. This article appeared in slightly different form as part of a symposium on James Welch in *American Indian Quarterly*, 4 May 1978.

"Blackfeet Winter Blues" from *Three American Literatures* by Kenneth Lincoln. Copyright © 1982 by Kenneth Lincoln. Reprinted and excerpted by permission of Kenneth Lincoln and the Modern Language Association.

"*The Death of Jim Loney:* Indian or Not?" by Kathleen Sands from *Studies in American Indian Literature.* Copyright © 1981 by Kathleen Sands. Reprinted by permission of Kathleen Sands.

This initial volume of The Confluence American Authors series was made possible, in part, by grants from The Idaho Commission on the Arts and The National Endowment for the Arts, Washington, D.C., a Federal Agency created by an act of Congress in 1965. This book constitutes a special edition of *The Slackwater Review.*

Series Design by Deborah L. Moloshok.
Production and typesetting by Linda Uhlenkott, Marilyn Heath, Joe Downs and Patricia Lackey.

About the Series

———————◆———————

The aim of this series is to present the best in contemporary critical opinion on modern and contemporary American authors alongside interviews, excerpts, bibliographies, letters, and manuscript selections. Initially, the present volume was planned and prepared as a special issue of *The Slackwater Review* to be published in the Spring of 1984. The change from magazine to book format permitted the inclusion of articles previously published with those originally commissioned, as well as the inclusion of more recent writing about James Welch. In this way, we believe the volume will make a more real and lasting contribution to American literary study, as will the succeeding volumes now in preparation. Our hope, then, is to focus critical attention on modern and contemporary American authors whose work merits serious attention, particularly those writers whose work recognizes that in *being* American our literature is intimately connected with a place. And that *that* place is a story that has already happened many times and is continuing to happen.

Consequently, the series also hopes to recognize what we believe is a vital but largely ignored link between the various literatures of the American continent, between, say, the poetry of Walt Whitman's "Song of Myself" and the Native American oral tradition. Or between James Welch's un-named narrator in *Winter in the Blood* and those anonymous narrators of primal myth, American Indian legends, stories, songs. All view their worlds in a similarly enchanted way. Each inhabits a peculiarly American place, and, likewise, each is uniquely concerned with an American identity. Each is in some way a recent immigrant. But then, so are all Americans, including the Blackfeet, especially when we reflect on time in relative terms, time chronological and geological, as opposed to time existential. Behind the idea for this series, then, is the corresponding idea that as Americans we live *in* time and through *it*, the rather radical idea (for

Americans anyway) that we *are* one nation and one people, united and indivisible by virtue of the very pluralism to which we owe our existence and by the place, the sacral ground, we hold in common. In short, behind the idea for this series is the assumption that all Americans build their huts in time's ruins just as surely as the Blackfeet once set up their lodges on soil once foreign to themselves and native to others, including badgers and buffalo.

James R. Hepworth, Series Editor

Preface

———◆———

Coincidentally, Keith Browning, recently retired editor of *Slackwater Review* and founder of Confluence Press, suggested that I edit a special issue on James Welch in the winter of 1983-84, the hundredth anniversary of the notorious Starvation Winter which old Yellow Calf recalls in *Winter in the Blood*. It has taken me a full year to complete the work, and in the interim Confluence Press has acquired a new managing editor, Jim Hepworth, whose assistance with the project has been valuable.

Jim Welch started as a poet and he plans to return to writing poems, probably after publication of his ambitious historical novel, now in progress. It was Welch's first novel, *Winter in the Blood* (1974), that brought him to prominence, not only through a number of enthusiastic reviews, but also because of a special issue of the *American Indian Quarterly*, (4 May 1978) devoted to a "symposium" on it. Contributors included several prominent critics and scholars now actively working on Native American literatures: Kathleen Sands, A. LaVonne Ruoff, Andrew Horton, Alan R. Velie.

From the *AIQ* symposium, we have reprinted Ruoff's impressive essay concerning women and alienation in *Winter in the Blood*. We have also added two original essays on the novel, Jack Davis' study of Indian identity and Robert Gish's examination of it as a novel of "mystery and mock intrigue."

Although the reviews of Welch's second novel, *The Death of Jim*

Loney (1979), were also quite positive, it has not gained so enthusiastic a following among critics and scholars. Accordingly, while it was easy to acquire several sound essays for this volume on *Winter in the Blood*, I found less extensive commentary on *The Death of Jim Loney*. We are pleased, however, to be able to reprint Kathleen Sand's fine essay from the Fall 1981 issue of *Studies in American Indian Literatures* on the "Indianness" of *The Death of Jim Loney*, and Dexter Westrum has supplied us with a valuable study of the mysterious bird that haunts the protagonist throughout the novel. The third essay I have contributed myself, with considerable trepidation. I have called upon two colleagues who are involved in Native American studies to act as readers of the manuscript, but no editor who publishes his own work should ever do so with any excess of confidence. In the process of preparing my essay, I became almost dreadfully conscious that I was a non-Indian male presuming to speak on the subject of Indian females. If my observations seem provocative on the one hand, or hare-brained on the other, I will content myself with the notion that they might at least attract to the novel the more serious attention I think it deserves.

Welch's poems, too, have been largely overlooked since the initial reviews of *Riding the Earthboy 40* (1971). Alan R. Velie's essay on Welch's surrealism has been recently recast in his book, *Four Indian Literary Masters* (1982), so I have opted to reprint Kenneth Lincoln's "Blackfeet Winter Blues," which offers a perceptive overview of the poems and is somewhat less narrow in its approach than Velie's observations. Two fresh essays on Welch's poetry, one by Peter Wild and another by Kim Stafford, both well-known poets in their own right, may stimulate further interest in the subject.

This volume is also intended to serve as an introduction to Welch himself and to the body of his work. To that end I have included an interview conducted by Keith Browning and me at Jim and Lois Welch's home in Missoula last spring. Among the photos we took that day, which will probably not prove worthy of printing, were covers of the various translations of Welch's novels: German (both East and West versions), Italian, Polish, and English editions of both novels. The artists' conceptions themselves constitute interpretations of a sort. This volume also contains ten poems from *Riding the Earthboy 40*, selections from both published novels, and a section of the new novel.

Finally, I have compiled a bibliography of works by and about James Welch. I wish I could promise that the bibliography is complete, but I have enough experience in such matters to know better than to make rash promises. I would welcome any notice as to omisssions, both great and small.

Our interview revealed that Welch is well aware of the critical response to his work, and that awareness places an especially heavy burden on the editor of a compilation like this one. No doubt Welch will read these essays and wince from time to time, but as Wallace Stevens once wrote, "fictive things/Wink as they will. Wink most when widows wince." The same goes for critical things.

Ron McFarland, 1984
University of Idaho

Contents

———◆———

Untitled Novel in Progress

Chronology

———————◆———————

1940   James Welch born, November 18, in Browning, Montana, a town of approximately two thousand located east of Glacier National Park. It serves as headquarters of the Blackfeet Reservation. He is Blackfeet on his father's side, Gros Ventre on his mother's.

1958   Graduated from Washburn High School in Minneapolis, having attended high schools on the Blackfeet and Fort Belknap reservations earlier.

1959   Attended University of Minnesota for two quarters.

1960-61   Worked on various jobs: natural gas pipeline in Minneapolis area, groundskeeper at a cemetery.

1961-62   Attended Northern Montana College in Havre.

1963-65   Attended University of Montana at Missoula, majoring in liberal arts and receiving the B.A. degree.

1965-67   Worked toward the M.F.A. degree at the University of Montana, studying with Richard Hugo and Madeline DeFrees. First poem published in *Voices International* (special Montana Poets issue), 1967.

1968	Married Lois Monk, now professor of comparative literatures at University of Montana.
1969	Received National Endowment for the Arts grant to work on his collection of poems.
1971	*Riding the Earthboy 40* (poems) published.
1972-73	Visited Greece, where he worked on second and final drafts of *Winter in the Blood.*
1974	*Winter in the Blood* (first novel) published.
1975	Won Pacific Northwest Booksellers Award for revised edition of *Riding the Earthboy 40.*
1976	*Riding the Earthboy 40* (revised edition published.
1977	Taught winter and spring quarters at University of Washington in the Theodore Roethke Chair.
1979	*The Death of Jim Loney* (novel) published. Appointed to the Montana State Board of Pardons.
1981	Began teaching regularly winter and spring quarters at University of Washington with joint appointment in Department of Indian Studies and Department of English. Received Indian Council Fire National Achievement Award and Montana Governor's Award.
1982-83	In San Miguel de Allende, Mexico, working on novel now in progress.
1984	Scheduled to teach at Cornell University during the spring semester. Plans to travel to Europe thereafter.

An Interview
with James Welch

———————◆———————

Interviewers Ron McFarland and M. K. Browning conducted the following interview on Saturday, February 4, 1984, in the Welch's dining room.

Ron McFarland: Is writing easy for you? Or as an alternative to that is writing easier now that you are working on your third novel than it once was?

Jim Welch: Well, yes, writing is definitely easier now. That much I can say for sure. But getting to the point of doing it is hard. Once I'm into a day to day rhythm, the writing seems to have its own momentum, just keeps going.

McFarland: You don't see yourself as writing by inspiration then? I think most people who write poetry—as you have done—something strikes them and they do it. Is it that way with a novel?

Welch: No, no. A novel is really, I think, in some ways, the easiest form of them all because you can write it day by day. It's not like a poem or a short story where you have to go several days thinking about it. With shorter forms, you just can't concentrate day by day; whereas, in a novel you can because you are thinking about the scene after that one. You're thinking about your characters. So every day you can write something on a novel.

Keith Browning: How far ahead do you think of the novel? Do you have the whole thing pretty much in mind before you start?

1

Welch: Yes. I do. I usually try to think about a book for about a year, and during that year, first of all, I think about the ending. Maybe, the ending won't come out the way I plan it, but I have to think that I know how it's going to end, because otherwise I'll get all balled up. Then I try to think of four or five high points in the novel—things that I can write toward. That way I can sort of trick myself and keep myself going if I can think that there is a high point fifty pages down the road. Then when I finish that one up, I can think, well, there's another one another fifty pages farther off. That way, I get over that boring, transitional kind of writing.

McFarland: Will you take notes as you go, or will this all be pretty much sustained in your head throughout the gestation period?

Welch: For about a year it will just remain in my head. When I'm mowing the lawn, or fishing, or something, I'll be thinking of characters and situations. Not so much about what the book is going to *mean* or anything like that, but just the technical aspects of the book. Then, at the end of that year, I'll probably make a few general notes. For the historical novel I'm writing, I had to make some specific historical notes to insure accuracy, enough so that nobody will be able to say, "This is absolutely wrong."

McFarland: I'm going to get back to that historical novel in a couple of minutes, but let me ask some more questions about your writing process. Do you have any kind of routine or ritual that you use when you are writing? Do you drink a lot of booze? Drink a lot of coffee? Eat a lot of apples? Smoke a lot?

Welch: It varies all the time. I think, for *The Death of Jim Loney,* I wrote from midnight till about four or five in the morning. But, that was just because I stayed up late, then, anyway, and so that was the best time. The house was quiet . . . because *everything* was quiet. I felt like I was just totally concentrating on the thing. This historical novel I'm writing in the afternoons. It just happens to work out that way. When I wrote *Winter in the Blood,* I wrote the second and third drafts in Greece. And I would spend from about ten o'clock at night 'til two in the morning writing, so the process always varies. The important thing, though, I think, if you are working on a long project like the novel, is that you've got to be there virtually every day.

Browning: You can't travel around much; you must stay and work on the thing?

Welch: Right. But I do travel too much. I get greedy. I want to get out there and make some money, and then it takes me a day or two to get ready to go on a trip and then when I come back, it takes me a couple of days to unwind, so it's really detrimental to go off from the project while I'm working on it.

McFarland: But you like to go off somewhere to write? You said you did a couple drafts of *Winter in the Blood* while you were in Greece. I know you went to Mexico while you were working on the new novel. Do you like to be away from your base when you write?

Welch: Yes. It seems to work out well. In Greece and Mexico—the language is foreign—so I did a lot less socializing. Out of a whole day a writer can only sightsee so much and go shopping so much. There's the rest of the day to be filled up—and it's perfect for writing.

Browning: How many drafts do you actually have to do?

Welch: Probably three complete drafts and then maybe go through it a fourth time for editing.

McFarland: Do you compose at the typewriter, or do you write it out in longhand first?

Welch: I used to compose poems by pencil, but I haven't written poems for quite some time now, and prose—it's just a lot easier to write it out on the typewriter because then you can see what you've got.

Browning: Let me ask that question another way. Clay Morgan, a young Idaho novelist, is hot for computers and word processors. He says they're the only way to go. Have you tried them?

Welch: Yes, Clay wrote me about that. A lot of people have attempted to sell me on the computer. The first person I ever heard of using one was Frank Herbert in Port Townsend. He swore by it... but, he's a computer himself. A day does not go by that Frank Herbert is not writing, so those things would really help him out. I don't think I'd use one, and I don't even know why. I know there is a terrific advantage to using one and that you can do all your drafts in one draft. Maybe that is the disadvantage. I like to see each draft on paper, but they say, "Hell, you can print it out at the end of the day," so that argument doesn't hold.

McFarland: Do you have a working title for this novel you're writing now?

Welch: No. I don't.

McFarland: Is thinking up a title the last thing you usually do?

Welch: Yes, it is. I know it's backwards, but it's from my poetry training. You know: you write the poem and then you title it afterwards. I'm just amazed that most people have a working title for a novel, virtually right from the beginning.

McFarland: What span in history is covered by your novel-in-progress on the Blackfeet?

Welch: It's just a three-year period—but a very important three-year period—from 1867 to 1870. Although the scope of the novel goes on beyond this, the culminating point is the Marias River massacre that occurred up here in which a band of Blackfeet got wiped out by the soldiers. Actually, the massacre was a case of mistaken identity. The soldiers were after a band led by Mountain Chief, but he'd moved out of this bend of the Marias. In the dead of winter in January, Heavy Runner's band had moved in, and so the soldiers snuck up on them at dawn in thirty-below weather and fired literally thousands of rounds into these lodges until finally they killed 173 people, including women and children. So the massacre became the major event of that period. During that winter, the Blackfeet were suffering from smallpox, which wiped out about a quarter of them. You know, they'd had about three major smallpox epidemics. So that was a big transitional period for them. After that massacre and after that winter of smallpox, they never took up arms against whites again. And before that period, they were noted for being great raiders of the plains.

McFarland: Is your novel going to try to deal with it from a multiple perspective, that is trying to flash back, here's the Indian side, here's the white side, and so forth? Or are you going to try to stay with the Blackfeet?

Welch: I'm staying exclusively with the Blackfeet. I'm trying to write from the inside-out, because most historical novels are written from the outside looking in. My main character is a member of a particular band, and I'm talking a lot about camp life and ceremonial life, those day to day practical things that they did to survive—and to live quite decently, as a matter of fact. So I'm writing it from the inside-out. The white people are the real strangers. They're the threatening presence out there all the time.

McFarland: Is your protagonist a historical character?

Welch: No, no. He's fictional and his band is fictional, but all the other bands are real, and I deal with real Blackfeet people, leaders, people like that. I wanted the freedom of making my main character and his band fictional so I would not feel constrained to follow any historical perspective.

Browning: You don't want to be held down by history?

Welch: That's right!

McFarland: Did you do extensive research on this, or what you would consider moderate research, or minimal research?

Welch: Well, I think most people would consider my efforts pretty minimal research. I read about five books, including Schultz.

Browning: You read J. W. Schultz?

Welch: Yes. Even though Schultz's period was a little after mine he still gives us a feeling for what the people were like, so I read him and I read about four other books. My Dad's grandmother had lived with him and survived that massacre on the Marias. She told him about that and several other things about the Blackfeet's lives before the whites. And *he* told *me* all these stories. At first that was my main idea, to just go by what my father had told me, but then I realized what I had to do, I had to set the novel in a period of history, I had to be faintly accurate. So that's why I read those books.

McFarland: Has having a factual, historical basis for your novel made analysis easier?

Welch: Much easier. Without a historical basis, you've got to really use your imagination, you've got to be thinking, "What am I going to do tomorrow? What is the next scene going to be like?" This one, because it is historical, you just follow A to B, to C, to D, and it virtually writes itself.

McFarland: History gives you a structure or a frame of reference automatically.

Welch: It gives you a structure, yes.

McFarland: Will your chapter structure be the same? Generally speaking, you write small chapters. Will you stick with that, what I think of as a trait of your style in fiction?

Welch: Pretty much so. Some of the scenes might be a little longer, but I think I will stick with that shorter format.

McFarland: I was wondering whether anyone has inquired about TV or movie rights for your other two novels?

Welch: Yes. In fact, *Winter in the Blood* had several options out on it, guys tried to make movies out of it; *The Death of Jim Loney*, I've had several inquiries about, but mostly from people who don't have the money. They want to tie up the book and then try to raise the money, that sort of thing. *The Death of Jim Loney* . . . it was actually a Broadway producer who was my best bite, a guy named Alexander Cohen. He managed the Shubert Theater. And he wanted to break into TV movies and my book was going to be the breaking in. We had a producer, we had a star, a director, and the whole thing. He was ready to go, but he just couldn't raise the money.

McFarland: So you would really like to do that, to see your novels become films?

Welch: Oh, yes, you're right.

McFarland: Well, I have a feeling that the one you're working on now might be the most likely of the three.

Welch: Yes, the novel-in-progress is almost an outline for a movie; if someone wanted to do a period movie, they could just follow the book because it's got a lot of drama, a lot of excitement built in, because it was set in that unique period of time.

McFarland: Yes, and a good director could film that with location shots and that kind of thing . . . In a sense the new novel might make a better film than either *Loney* or *Winter in the Blood.*

Welch: Yes, I think they both had some cinematic qualities, but they were too quiet. Nobody wants to take a chance of making a quiet movie.

McFarland: Can we talk more about the structure of your novels, what would be called an "episodic structure"? When I first picked up one of your novels and read it, I thought, "Boy! Why haven't I read any of Welch's short stories?" So far as I can tell, you don't write short stories. Am I right?

Welch: No. No, I don't write stories.

McFarland: Have you ever? I mean, in a classroom setting?

Welch: In a class, I wrote short stories. That would have been back in '63 or something like that.

McFarland: So, why don't you? Just because there's no money in it?

Welch: That's probably part of it, anyway. It seems like poetry and novels cover the whole thing. And it seems like short stories would be just another form to dilute your energy, and I don't think I would be particularly good at short story writing. Toby Wolf is really good, Ray Carver is really good. They think in those terms. But I don't know, I can't even imagine how you have to think in order to write short stories. I like the idea of thinking of this long work that you can deal with—as you say—episodically. You can attack it like that and then you tie the whole structure together and you've got a novel. You've also got a way to make a little money as a result. But short stories just don't appeal to me.

Browning: They would be actually harder to write than the novel, wouldn't they?

Welch: I'm convinced that they are. If you wrote the equivalent of a novel, it would probably be twelve short stories. And could you imagine having to think up a new idea every single time and execute it, whereas in a novel you think up one idea, and the whole thing is an execution of that idea.

McFarland: Your first book was a collection of poetry, but I've seen nothing since. Does that mean you have given up on poetry, finished with it? I noticed in the interview with Bill Bevis in *Northwest Review* that you mentioned something about a general notion of writing some prose poems somewhere down the line.

Welch: I'm still thinking of writing those prose poems.

McFarland: So you expect that when you do go back to poetry that, at least initially, your style will have changed a good bit from what you were doing before?

Welch: Yes.

McFarland: Well, I was just curious, since the reviews on the poems were mixed, what it would be like to write fiction for quite a while and go back. Surely your perspective on poetry will have changed or altered in some way. I will be interested to see what will happen.

Welch: I hope I will be smarter when I go back.

McFarland: Do you have any sense of how your work goes over with Indians in general, or with Blackfeet and Gros Ventres and so forth in particular?

Welch: As a matter of fact, Indian people really seem to like my work. It amazes me, because I keep expecting somebody to say, "You're exploiting Indians," or "exploiting a quality of Indians, like drinking and you shouldn't be, because you are painting a bad picture of Indians." And I've had about two people tell me that in my entire writing career, two Indian people. But that didn't bother me, because the majority of them feel that I paint pictures of reservation life as it really is. And that is really nice. People, especially up at the Fort Belknap Reservation, Indians in Montana particularly, say that I write the truth. I would hate to have the people who are the most important people tell me that I'm doing it wrong.

McFarland: Or, to simply read it and say, "well I know that it is very artistic, but frankly, I just do not understand. I mean, this must be too literary for me" or something like that. That would be painful, to realize that while the New York reviewers were fawning over it that somehow it was not communicating to—

Welch: —that you were writing to a different group of people. It is interesting to me that those people do accept it, but more importantly, *they* can also be critical. Like I've had Indian people tell me, "Well, why don't you write any books with a happy ending?"

McFarland: The universal complaint.

Welch: Right, and you know those who have literary backgrounds say the same thing about Momaday or Silko. They say, "Why don't Indian authors write about situations that have a happy ending or a positive ending?" I'd say most of the Indian experience isn't happy or positive, so we are reflecting that. But I do expect that some day somebody is going to come along and write . . .

McFarland: . . . the great Indian comic novel.

Welch: Right.

McFarland: A thousand laughs?

Welch: At least a happy ending.

McFarland: Critics have commented on several comic aspects of *Winter in the Blood* . . . Charles Larson and Andrew Horton and Alan Velie, and others. I haven't read all the comments on *Loney*, but I realize most of the critics are not going to be writing about the comic aspects. I wonder if *Loney* was a completion of a kind of vision? Here was *Winter in the Blood*, with a broadly construed comic perspective in some ways as opposed to *Loney*, which would be tragic, the dark side so to speak. Do you think of *Winter in the Blood* as being a comic novel?

Welch: Yes, I was happy that people saw the humor in it. And it's interesting that many people, I've discovered, are afraid to laugh with that book, and I can't understand why. They think it's Indians and they think it's about alienation and so on and, therefore, there should be no funny moments in the novel. But I intentionally put comic stuff in there just to alleviate that vision of alienation and purposelessness, aimlessness, whereas in *The Death of Jim Loney*, by the very nature of its subject, there could be very little comedy. The guy is going to kill himself. No, that's not too funny.

McFarland: I noticed that when the reviewers raved about *Winter in the Blood* they were already talking about the balance in the novel, even *before* a lot of the scholars got hold of it, as in the *American Indian Quarterly* special issue on *Winter in the Blood.* How fortuitous it was and how this was just the right kind of thing, and then Jim Loney came in and although I have not read too many of the reviews on it, I've talked to some people who teach Native American Literature courses. They feel that it's hard to teach *Jim Loney;* they do like teaching *Winter in the Blood* very much, but to them *Jim Loney* is down, too dark.

Welch: Too dark. I know a lot of people feel that way, but I don't. People write to me who say they have taught it and have had interesting responses to it. Maybe it's not as much fun to teach as *Winter in the Blood*, but the responses to it are interesting.

McFarland: I think it was in Bevis' interview that something came up relative to the end of *The Death of Jim Loney,* whether or not the end was to be considered completely catastrophic. Something like that. And I believe your point at the time *was* that there was some moment of redemption to give life some meaning, and, in a way, he seizes upon this accidental killing—which I don't think *is* quite obviously an accident. It could have been either one.

McFarland: Yes. I think so, too. But some will suppose that . . .

Welch: Yes. Some people do think of it as just an accidental death, and they say, "Well, why didn't Loney just give himself up?" They are exasperated. They want it to make sense. To be logical.

Browning: There is no guilt involved in Loney's charting?

Welch: Just a kind of nominal guilt for having killed this guy, but I think Loney turns it back on himself then. I think Loney's killing this guy is a reflection on his whole life and the reason that he does what he does after killing this guy is to carry his life through to its completion. I think the novel is about looking back and looking forward, trying to make some sense of it all. Loney can't see anything beyond this death, the death of himself. So that is why it is important for him to carry it through, to make sure.

McFarland: This might be seen as Loney's perspective, his justice. His sense of justice requires that he die, not so much in expiation of sin or something, *so much* as for a very simple sense of justice; I think that he is a deep enough character to speculate or realize that his killing of Myron Pretty Weasel is, as a matter of fact, murder. If not in first degree, maybe in the second degree, half degree murder, that is only partly accidental.

Welch: Yes, and then Loney increasingly makes it a murder in his own mind. So, finally, he comes to think, "I did murder Pretty Weasel and therefore, the same should happen to me."

McFarland: If I understand correctly, when Loney looks back into his past, investigates his past, he does not make the kind of discovery that is made in *Winter in the Blood.*

Welch: That's right. Think of Loney's sister. He can't understand her. His sister is able to just forget about her past and just think of the future. He can't forget about his past, and he can't make any discoveries about his past.

Browning: No epiphanies.

Welch: No epiphanies. Exactly. Whereas in *Winter in the Blood,* the narrator has a giant epiphany. You know, "this is my grandfather."

McFarland: And all because the horse farted. That's actually a classic kind of epiphany in a Joycean kind of sense, to be triggered by something very trivial.

Welch: Something vulgar. I enjoyed doing that scene a lot. And I hope that in this historical novel I can get back to some of that, some funny scenes.

McFarland: I used to ask a colleague of mine who teaches Native American Literature what Indian humor is like, why we don't see much Indian humor, or whether there is an Indian sense of humor. At that time I think I had finished reading Silko's *Ceremony,* and prior to that I had read some of Momaday's work, and I was thinking of my earliest sense of more or less serious cinematography, like the Ira Hayes story, of the oppressive alcoholism, and the isolation and alienation. I wondered, "Is it always this way for Indian people? Is there no sense of humor here at all? Are these people always grim?" There is always a sort of picture, like those of Sitting Bull or Geronimo, and these men are always very fierce looking and not very happy people—for obvious reasons. "Is there any Indian humor at all?" And my friend used to say, "Well, there are the coyote stories, but it's a different sort of humor."

Welch: And there is the teasing. Indians are notorious for teasing each other and that really generates the humor. But that is the kind of stuff that really is hard to put down in writing. I've been in trailer houses full of Indians and there would be all this teasing going on and the walls practically coming down because everybody is laughing so hard. But if you were to record it and then write down exactly what was said, a lot of times it would be hard to find out what was so funny.

McFarland: Because you would have to know the character of the person, because that is what is being teased, in some ways? Is that it?

Welch: Yes, right, and then the way that person reacts to the teasing.

A lot of Indian humor is very witty, really witty, plays on words and so on. But it is interesting. It would be an interesting experience to see if you could transcribe that, an evening like that, into print, if there would be anything at all funny.

McFarland: Well, it's interesting that you mentioned the verbal element, because one might suggest that Western European wit *which* is largely verbal play and that sort of thing . . .

Welch: Yes. Yes.

McFarland: . . . and in that respect the humor is often transcribable, in that respect it constitutes a verbal joke, one that is actually set up and constructed and offered as a verbal joke, even somewhat as we were talking the other night, the NoDak joke. A lot of Western wit in literature is like that. My sense of it is that Indian humor is not *that* kind of verbal humor anyhow.

Welch: No, it's not. But, we do have the formal jokes. Someone will say, "Did you hear the one about . . ." yes, and if you read that joke, it would be funny, still, if you read some of the Indian humor that goes on amongst Indian people, you'd have a hard time pointing your finger at something that was really funny. I never have heard people laugh as hard or as loud as I have heard when I'm in a roomful of Indian people and they are telling these things, just teasing each other. And I've never laughed so hard either when it was going on. It's really contagious.

McFarland: I noticed in the living room a Dutch translation of *Jim Loney,* and I thought how curious that it could appeal to Blackfeet readers on the one hand, and yet, at the same time appeal, not just to New York reviewers, but also to Europeans. I was excited to see that translation and also to realize that there was a Dutch translation of *Winter in the Blood.* What are the other foreign languages that your work has been translated into?

Welch: German, both East and West, Italian . . .

McFarland: Both novels?

Welch: German for *Winter in the Blood,* Italian versions of both novels, Polish and then British.

McFarland: A special British edition?

Welch: Yes. If you think the cover for *The Death of Jim Loney* in the American edition is funny, you should see the British edition: a kind of punk-rocker Indian hanging onto a wire fence.

McFarland: Maybe in the British version, instead of Jim Loney drinking Thunderbird wine or whatever, he actually drinks sherry?.. I wonder about your family. You mentioned your father being an influence in some ways. What does your father do, or what did he do? He's retired now I gather.

Welch: He retired. He's done many things in his life. He's a real Renaissance man. He could weld, and he worked for the Indian Service, in fact, he ran a TB sanitarium up in Alaska, and he's worked as an administrator in hospitals. When he retired a couple years ago he was ranching and farming. He really did a lot of different things. He's from Browning; he's Blackfeet. I just got a family tree of his side of the family which is fantastic.

McFarland: How far back does it go?

Welch: To about 1830. There was a Spaniard who came up named Sandoval. He came up from New Mexico in 1830, and he guided Prince Maximilian and Maxwell Bodener when they came into this country. I have a lot of famous relatives. Malcolm Clark was a famous person who dealt with Indians, he took a Blackfeet wife, and, in a sense, triggered the massacre on the Marias. A man named Altra went down and killed Malcolm Clark for having insulted him. And *that* is what really angered the white folks and eventually resulted in this massacre. Clark was a relative of mine. Then there is an ancestor of mine named Richard Sanderville... he changed his family name from Sandoval to Sanderville and thought he was Anglicizing it, but he was actually Frenchifying it. But he is an historian, who did a lot of winter counts for old Blackfeet warriors. They would want their exploits recorded, and he even developed a kind of shorthand. Certain things like upside-down-horseshoes meant *raids*, and he had shorthand for Crow and all of that. So he made winter counts for these old warriors and grew to be a highly respected historian. All the white historians always went to him to find out about the life. So that's my dad's side of the family.

Browning: Do you write from what you have experienced? How true is your work to personal experience?

Welch: A lot of people thought that *Winter in the Blood* was autobiographical because certain incidents happened to me—like getting punched out in an Indian bar, waking up against a parking meter—certain things like that. But basically, the novel is not autobiographical, although the ranch setting was our ranch. I just used the buildings and the topography, and so on.

McFarland: And Jim Loney's athletic exploits are undoubtedly your own!

Welch: Oh, yes!

Browning: I can just see you out there at the top of the key.

Welch: I used to play both "horse" and "21" when we lived out at Roseacres. We had a basket on the back of an old barn up there and Dick Hugo would come up. In the beginning, I'd always beat him all the time because I had a good outside shot, and, of course, I was mobile enough to get the ball so that I could make the short shot close to the basket. After a while, he got real deadly and our games got closer all the time and more serious as a result.

McFarland: But let's not leave out your mother. She was Gros Ventre? Is there any stigma attached to marrying outside your tribe? Nowadays? I suppose there might have been in the 1870's, maybe even not then, I don't know.

Welch: No, I think it is interesting, I think it *is* a misconception about Indians, which was based on a reality way back in the old days. If you brought a Crow woman into the group, she would most likely have been a captive and would have been treated that way. Our women loved captive women because they would do all the gruntwork. But eventually that Crow woman would have married into the Blackfeet and would have tried to become a very respected member of the group. And so, in the twentieth century, there has been a lot of marriage between people of the Blackfeet from the Fort Belknap Reservation where the Gros Ventres and Assiniboines are and the Fort Peck Reservation where the Sioux are, and even down to the Crow and Cheyenne people. There has been a lot of intermarriage between those.

McFarland: What did your mother do?

Welch: She worked all her life. She went to Haskell, which is an

Indian school down in Kansas, and learned secretarial skills. She was a stenographer, one of the old timers who really knew how to take shorthand and do all that kind of work. Then she worked at that virtually all her life, on various reservations and Indian communities.

McFarland: Do you have brothers and sisters, or are you an only child?

Welch: I have two brothers. My older brother is a forester down in California, and my younger brother is the farmer up on the highline.

McFarland: Does he farm a family allotment up there?

Welch: He farms my mother's land. They live on the Fort Belknap Reservation. She had some land that they farm, but they have also been buying land throughout the years. They actually have two farms, one the old ranch and a big dry-land wheat farm out in the hills. My brother leases a lot of land from people who don't have the wherewithal to break it up and plant it.

McFarland: That leads me in some kind of curious way to the Indian family unit, the extended family idea. In your novels, at least so far, the families seem to be rather strange, and even in *Winter in the Blood*, where the extended family is still there to some extent, it seems to me that there is a kind of distance. Maybe it's because the characters themselves have this alienation. In *The Death of Jim Loney*, the family is practically obliterated except for this ghost-like father. It's really peculiar and I was wondering: is this becoming a common thing in reservation experience, that the family is under pressure, disintegrating?

Welch: I think there are always people who isolate themselves from their families. In a way, I am thinking about my dad's family. They were really close knit, he and his brother and sisters and my grandparents on his side, and all of the relatives that we have up around Browning. They were all real relatives, no matter how shirttail they were. So that was a real extended family on his side. Now, on my mom's side, it was always circumscribed. They didn't have this kind of openness—"Hey there's my cousin over there!" —or whatever. Anybody that walks down the street: "That's my cousin, you know, on my dad's side." There were certain set relatives. They didn't claim everybody.

McFarland: So, they weren't shattered families of the sort you see in Jim Loney?

Welch: No. They weren't shattered families. I guess I was saying that in my family's generation the family unit was still really strong. In my generation, it seems that it is starting to break down. There are a lot of Indian people who isolate themselves and fend off any other people, and then there are sons who go away and try to forget that they came from the reservation. The family is breaking down.

Browning: What will happen, eventually, to the Indian families? Will they keep shattering, bring on further alienation, isolation, recede into the background of American history?

Welch: I think it depends on which group of Indians we are talking about. Obviously, the Navahos are going to go on for a long, long time, because they have such a vast reservation that they can still maintain their culture. The Sioux reservations in the Dakotas are still very strong, but some of the reservations in Montana are eventually going to change. The people are going to be getting further and further away from their culture, so actually the reservation will be just a place to live. There will always be Indians, but they won't be very traditional, I don't think, on these small reservations.

Browning: What about the ones that have turned mercantile, like the Warm Springs Indians? It's like a big resort that they're running. They have a battery of lawyers that work for them. They are making money.

Welch: Yes, well, maybe the tribes themselves won't die out. The tribe is a political unit. I think that will still be there.

Browning: Well the Nez Perce have a very strong sense of their tribal politics. They have a governing committee, tribal council.

Welch: Yes, they were pretty smart right from the beginning, weren't they?

Browning: One of their leaders, though, I don't think he was actually one, was called Lawyer.

McFarland: Do you ever see yourself writing a novel that would not be from your Indian experience and your personal background? Do you ever see yourself doing something altogether different? You know: you go down to Mexico and see some completely different experience you have to write. Do you ever see yourself doing that?

Welch: Yes. Now that you mention it, when I was down there in Mexico I could see myself possibly writing a novel about Mexican life, but it would probably be told from an outsider's point of view because I couldn't presume to speak from the Mexican standpoint. I am on the Parole Board here in Montana, and we go to the prison every month for these meetings, interviews for prisoners. I've often thought, prisoners have the most fantastically interesting backgrounds that you can possibly imagine. We go through probably eighty cases a month, and each one of them is incredible. So, I often think, "God, I'd like to write a novel about this experience," but I don't know which point of view I would tackle—the member of the parole board?—or would it be the prison situation?—or would it be an inmate's standpoint? So, although I wouldn't know how to go about that, I could conceive of writing a novel based upon that experience, which wouldn't be my own or my background.

McFarland: If you had not become a writer or teacher and achieved success of some sort in both areas, do you have any sense of what you might have done? Like to have been? Or what you might have been whether you had liked it or not?

Welch: Really hard to say. I started out in business administration when I first went to college, thinking that I'd like to own my own store some day or whatever, but I couldn't do the bookkeeping or the math involved. I think you start finding things that you can't do. As I said, my older brother is a forester, but that requires a lot of education. My younger brother is a farmer, so maybe I could have ended up being a farmer or something like that.

McFarland: When did you start writing? Did you start writing when you were nine or ten? Did you discover your talent right away?

Welch: No. Actually, I had two periods of writing. One was probably in late high school, you know how you write rhyming poems to cheerleaders, that kind of thing. But I actually started writing and took it very seriously when I got into Dick Hugo's workshop. Well, it was the Winter Quarter of 1966. I've been at it seriously from then on.

McFarland: But it was poetry at first wasn't it?

Welch: It was probably even more than poetry. It was probably just Hugo's personality. He made us all seem like, "God, it's possible to be a human being and a poet at the same time."

McFarland: When did the fiction come in? Was there someone in particular there? Or was that just a genre?

Browning: Was that Bill Kitteridge?

Welch: Well, Kitteridge sure helped me, but actually I wrote fiction on my own. I felt that at one point I was just not doing it. I was writing short lyrical poems and I wanted to get something, a piece of writing where I could capture the whole country and have some people in it.

Browning: A bigger canvas.

Welch: A bigger canvas, yes. So on my own I wrote the first draft of *Winter in the Blood,* and then Bill Kitteridge read it. I had him read it to offer me some criticism, thinking he would praise most of it, maybe write a little bit of criticism ... Every single page he went through had red marks all over it. And, we sat down one night for six hours or so, going page by page, and by the end of that night I thought, to hell with it. I am never writing prose again. He really broke my heart, so I put it away. I said, "This is it, I tried prose and it didn't work." Then about a month later I pulled it out, and I could see that he was right, in virtually every single comment, and it actually made my rewriting job that much easier, because it had been so thoroughly criticized.

McFarland: Did you do a lot of tightening up? Was it that kind of thing?

Welch: I always had a sense of economy from my poetry background. It wasn't so much that I was blathering on, but it was like some scenes just weren't right for that book. For example, I had a scene about a cycle of ranch life, the four seasons and what it means to a rancher. I really wanted to get that in, but once I did, it didn't fit. It had no place in that novel. And he taught me things like dialogue. I didn't know how to do dialogue. My beginning dialogues were very wooden, people speaking directly to each other back and forth. Kitteridge taught me a simple little trick, that people talk over each others' shoulders. They are always just a little off. Once he pointed things like that out to me, it made sense. I don't think my style changed much from that early, terrible draft; it was just getting it all together and trying to figure out what makes a novel. What should be dramatic and how does dialogue work? Just some of the technical tricks of writing.

McFarland: Do you see yourself staying in Missoula? What would it take to uproot you?

Welch: I can't imagine leaving Missoula. I do like to get away. We have taken trips years away, and I go out to Seattle every spring quarter to teach at the University of Washington, which is a nice little break from Missoula.

Browning: How many years have you been doing that?

Welch: Since '76 or '77—something like that.

McFarland: So you would like to keep on doing that kind of thing?

Welch: Yes. I like to get out of Missoula, but I also like to come back to Missoula. I know this town, I know the country around it, I know all the rivers, I know where the fish are.

McFarland: Are there any fish in that creek back of your house?

Welch: Back there, you betcha. Kids catch fish out of there all the time. Kid next door here from behind our house to the end of the block caught something like twenty fish.

McFarland: Were they little cutthroats?

Welch: Yes. Little cutthroats, rainbows. He had a couple that were probably fourteen inches.

McFarland: Got a fishing pole?

Winter
in the
Blood

from
Winter in the Blood

◆

Lame Bull had taken to grinning now that he was a proprietor. All day he grinned as he mowed through the fields of alfalfa and bluejoint. He grinned when he came in to lunch, and in the evening when the little tractor putted into the yard next to the granary, we could see his white teeth through the mosquito netting that hung from his hat brim. He let his whiskers grow so that the spiky hair extended down around his round face. Teresa complained about his sloppy habits, his rough face. She didn't like the way he teased the old lady, and she didn't like his habit of not emptying the dust and chaff in his pants cuffs. He grinned a silent challenge, and the summer nights came alive in the bedroom off the kitchen. Teresa must have liked his music.

We brought in the first crop, Lame Bull mowing alfalfa, snakes, bluejoint, baby rabbits, tangles of barbed wire, sometimes changing sickles four times in a single day. Early next morning he would be down by the granary sharpening the chipped, battered sickles. He insisted on both cutting and baling the hay, so my only job was the monotonous one of raking it into strips for the baler. Around and around I pulled the windrow rake, each circuit shorter than the last as I worked toward the center. I sat on the springy seat of the Farmall, which was fairly new, and watched Lame Bull in the next field. He tinkered endlessly with the baler, setting the tension tighter so that the bales would be more compact, loosening it a turn when they began to break. Occasionally I would see the tractor idling, the regular puffs of black smoke popping from its stack, and Lame Bull's legs sticking out from beneath the baler. He enjoyed being a proprietor and the haying went smoothly until we hired Raymond Long Knife to help stack bales.

Long Knife came from a long line of cowboys. Even his mother, perhaps the best of them all, rode all day, every day, when it came time to round up the cattle for branding. In the makeshift pen, she wrestled calves, castrated them, then threw the balls into the ashes of the branding fire. She made a point of eating the roasted balls while glaring at one man, then another—even her sons, who, like the rest of us, stared at the brown hills until she was done.

Perhaps it was because of this fierce mother that Long Knife had become shrewd in the way dumb men are shrewd. He had learned to give the illusion of work, even to the point of sweating as soon as he put his gloves on, while doing very little. But because he was Belva Long Knife's son and because he always seemed to be hanging around the bar in Dodson, he was in constant demand.

The day we hired him the weather changed. It was one of those rare mid-July days when the wind blows chilly through the cotton-woods and the sky seems to end fifty feet up. The ragged clouds were both a part of and apart from the grayness; streaks of white broke suddenly, allowing sun to filter through for an instant as the clouds closed and drove swiftly north.

Lame Bull of course drove the bull rake, not because he was best at it but because it was the proprietor's job. He wore his down vest and his sweat-stained pearl stetson pulled low over his big head. Although he was thick and squat, half a head shorter than either Teresa or I, he had a long torso; seated on the bull rake, which was mounted on stripped-down car frame, he looked like a huge man, but he had to slide forward to reach the brake and clutch pedals.

He lowered the rake and charged the first row of bales. The teeth skimmed over the stubble, gathering in the bales; then the proprietor pulled back a lever and the teeth lifted. He swerved around to deliver the bales at our feet. We began to build the stack.

By noon we had the first field cleared. Things went smoothly enough those first two days as we moved from field to field. Long Knife and I built the stacks well, squaring off the corners, locking each layer in place with the next one so that the whole wouldn't lean, or worse, collapse. The cloudy weather held steady those days, at times trying to clear up, at other times threatening a downpour. But the weather held and Lame Bull was happy. He gazed lovingly at each stack we left behind us.

The third day there was not a cloud in the sky. We didn't work that morning in order to give the bales a chance to dry out. Although it hadn't rained, the humidity and dew had dampened them just enough so that they might spoil if we tried to stack them right away. After lunch Long Knife and I drove out to the field in the pickup. Lame Bull had broken two teeth on the bull rake and screwed up the hydraulic lift, so he followed us with the tractor and hay wagon. We would have to pick the bales by hand, which meant a long hard afternoon. In the rearview mirror I could see Lame Bull's grinning face, partially hidden behind the tractor's chimney. Long Knife leaned out of the cab window and turned his face to the sky. It was a small round face with a short sharp nose and tiny slanted eyes. They called him Chink because of those eyes. He was a tall man, slender, with just the beginnings of a paunch showing above his belt buckle. On the silver face of the buckle was a picture of a bucking horse and the words: *All-around Cowboy, Wolf Point Stampede, 1954*. The buckle was shiny and worn from scraping against the bars of taverns up and down the valley. He was not called Chink to his face because of the day he almost beat the Hutterite to death with that slashing buckle.

"Jesus, beautiful, ain't it?" he said.

I nodded, but he was still looking out the window. I said, "You bet."

"How much does Lame Bull owe me?"

"Two days—twenty bucks so far."

Long Knife continued to gaze out the window. To the north, just above the horizon, we could see the tail end of the two-day run of clouds.

"Twenty bucks—that ain't much for two days' work, is it?"

I didn't say anything.

"It's enough, though . . . By God, it's enough." He sounded as though he had made a great decision. "How much is he paying you?"

"Same thing—ten bucks a day."

"That sure ain't much." He was still leaning out the window. As he shook his head, his black hair bristled against his shirt collar.

We crossed the dry irrigation ditch. This was the last field, but the alfalfa grew thickest here and the bales were scarcely ten feet apart. I killed the motor. I could hear Long Knife's hair bristling against his collar as he continued to shake his head. We waited for Lame Bull to catch up.

He stopped the tractor beside the pickup and grinned at us as we climbed out. "You throw 'em up," he said to me. "Raymond will stack 'em—ain't it, Raymond?"

Long Knife looked uncomfortable. I could tell what was coming, but Lame Bull continued to grin. I walked over to a bale beside the wagon and threw it on. I heard Long Knife say something, but the noise of the idling tractor obscured it. I walked around the wagon and threw another bale on. Lame Bull leaned down toward Long Knife: "You what?" I threw another bale on. "You heard me!" I walked behind the wagon to the pickup. I took a drink from the water bag. "You heard me!"

Lame Bull popped the clutch on the tractor. It lurched forward and died. He stepped down and checked the hitch on the wagon. Then he walked to the front of the tractor and kicked the tire. "Remind me to put some more air in this one," he said.

Long Knife kicked one of the big rear tires and nodded. I put the cap on the water bag and hung it on the door handle. Lame Bull had his back to us. He was grinning at the field full of bales. I could tell.

"Look, you give me a ride back to town and I'll buy you a beer," Long Knife said.

I avoided his eyes. I didn't want to be his ally.

Long Knife turned to Lame Bull: "But look at my hands—they're cut and bleeding. Do you want me to get infected?"

Lame Bull refused to look at his hands. "I'll pay your doctor bills when we're through."

"My head is running in circles with this heat."

"I'll pay for your head too."

"We better get started," I said, but no one moved. I sat down on the running board.

"Look at my hands."

I looked at his hands. It was true that they were raw from throwing around the bales. One finger was actually cut.

"You did that last night on one of those movie magazines," I said. "Besides, you should have wore gloves like the rest of us."

Long Knife folded his arms and leaned against the rear fender of the pickup. It was clear that he wasn't going to work anymore, no matter what happened. We were wasting time and I wanted to get the field cleared. It was the last field.

"Listen to me, Lame Bull—let's let him go. You and me'll work twice as hard and when it's done, it's done."

My logic seemed to impress Long Knife. "Listen to him, Lame Bull."

Lame Bull didn't listen. He wasn't listening to anybody. I could tell that, as his eyes swept the field, he was counting bales, converting them into cows and the cows into calves and the calves into cash.

"You can't keep me here against my will. You have to pay me and let me go back to town."

"Listen, Lame Bull—you have to pay him," I said.

"You're damn right," Long Knife said.

"And let him go back to town."

"You tell him, boy."

"He ain't a slave, you know."

There was a pause. I could see the highway from where I sat, but there were no cars. Beyond the highway, the Little Rockies seemed even tinier than their name.

Without turning around, Lame Bull pulled out his sweaty hand-carved wallet, took out a bill, crumpled it into a ball and threw it over his head. It landed at our feet.

"That's more like it," Long Knife said, smoothing out the bill. It was a twenty. "You going to give me a ride, boy?"

"I don't have a car."

"You could take the pickup here."

"It isn't mine. It belongs to Teresa," I said.

"But she's your mother." Long Knife was getting desperate.

"She's his wife," I said, looking at Lame Bull's back. "Why don't you ask him for a ride?"

Long Knife thought about this for a minute. He pushed his hat back on his head. "I'll give you two dollars," he said, as though he had just offered Lame Bull a piece of the world. "Two dollars and a beer when we get to town."

The magpie floating light-boned through the afternoon air seemed to stop and jump straight up when Lame Bull's fist landed. Long Knife's head snapped back as he slammed into the pickup, his hat flying clear over the box. It was a sucker punch, straight from the shoulder, delivered with a jump to reach the taller man's nose.

"Jesus Christ almighty!" I said, leaping from the spray of blood.

Lame Bull was not grinning. He picked up Long Knife and threw him in the back of the pickup. "Get in," he said. I retrieved the hat—the sweatband was already wet—and climbed into the cab. Lame Bull had wrapped a blue bandanna around his hand. With shifting gears and whining motor, the pickup shot off across the fields toward the highway.

"You might have to get a tetanus shot for that hand," I said, looking through the back window at Long Knife, his face smeared with blood, his little eyes staring peacefully up at the clear blue sky.

Restoration of
Indian Identity in
Winter in the Blood

———————◆———————

Jack L. Davis

In 1890, nearly 400 years after Columbus opened the new world to European invasion, the military conquest of American Indians was completed when Custer's old command, the seventh cavalry division, massacred Big Foot's surrendering band of Lakotas at Wounded Knee. That slaughter forever ended armed resistance and all surviving "hostiles" were located upon their reservations. Most observers predicted that the redman would soon vanish from the face of the earth or completely meld into the burgeoning white population.

For the next 60 years, the federal government did its best to eradicate remaining tribal culture, convinced that Indians had no future as Indians. Reservations were divided into individual allotments to break down the extended family into nuclear units and to destroy the village practice of holding land communally. Tribal governance based on consensus was replaced by Anglo-style politics, which created factionalism and permitted partisan groups with slight majorities to dominate the entire tribe. Tribal unity was further fragmented when missionaries of antithetical persuasions were unleashed to compete for converts and to help abolish traditional religious ceremonies. Indian children were torn from their homes and sent for civilizing to distant boarding schools where they were prohibited from speaking their mother tongues. Meanwhile, back on the reservations, adults were forced into alien modes of subsistence, European farming and herding practices, with which they often had little experience and less sympathy. Finally, in the 1950's the Eighty-Third Congress devised the ultimate solution to the Indian problem as they began to legislate Indians out of existence by abolishing treaties that guaranteed already dwindling land bases. As the Klamath and Menominee reservations first fell under the Eisenhower administration's termination policy, the death knell for American Indians seemed sounded throughout the nation.

Yet, the process of extinguishing Indians unaccountably failed. Instead, scattered and submerged resistance movements finally cohered and surfaced in the late sixties, when Indian activists, often led by returned war veterans, exploded into uncharacteristic militancy that culminated in the occupation of Alcatraz, the fishing rights victory in Washington state, the seizure of BIA headquarters in Washington, D.C., and the highly symbolic recapture of the village of Wounded Knee early in 1973. These rebellions served notice that some Indians had neither disappeared nor assimilated. In fact, by then the decimated native population had almost regained its aboriginal level of perhaps 850,000.[1] How this feat of ethnic survival has been achieved, despite overwhelming odds, is still not well understood. Somehow, reservation societies, which appeared to be assimilating, were instead taking over many Euro-American traits and institutions but placing them into a tribal context, thereby preserving a distinctively Indian personality and life style. While many Indians thus acculturated without assimilating, others, of course, did not. Thousands went to the cities, where some retained ethnic identities but others disappeared into the national melting pot.

Anthropologists like A. Irving Hallowell and George D. Spindler, who pioneered exacting studies of the machanics of acculturation and assimilation, discovered that transforming Indians into whites was not a simple, accretionary process. Hallowell analyzed two closely related tribal groups—one adhering to aboriginal hunting, fishing, and trapping lifeways and the other almost indistinguishable from their white neighbors in language, dress, and occupation. Yet he found, contrary to all expectations, "a persistent core of psychological characteristics sufficient to identify an Objiway personality configuration"[2] among both groups. The tribe considered by whites as assimilated, in fact, continued to refer to themselves as Indians. Likewise Spindler, who exhaustively examined the Menominee and Blood, discovered that acculturation proceeded smoothly only in those rare cases when

Indian and white personality traits converged. Generally natives viewed white culture as confronting their tribal identity, threatening the way they perceived the world. To maintain cognitive control, Indians either: (1) selected only synthesizable elements, (2) adopted conflicting elements under duress and kept them rigidly segmented from the Indian cognitive world, or (3) simply abandoned the tribal world for the new psychocultural system. Interestingly, Spindler added that too direct a confrontation between Indian and white cognitive systems can entirely destroy mental control. The embattled individual then "has no ability to predict, to plan, to choose, to put first things first, to keep his wits about him."[3] As these studies indicate, the popular belief that Indians would gradually assimulate through progressive acculturation of specific elements from white culture (language, education, and economic pursuits) has no basis in fact. Whether one is Indian or white depends primarily upon the configurating cognitive perspective from which one perceives the world, understands it, and acts within it. In between, exists a limbo of nonidentity.

However, as the distinguished Indian anthropologist D'Arcy McNickle pointed out, it is hard to get from scientific analyses any clear picture of how specific people respond to the pressures threatening their ethnic identity.[4] To do that, he turned to the novel, believing that in the concrete dramatizations of individual personalities permitted by imaginative fiction, the reader can better grasp the mechanics by which an alien mentality and culture is accommodated or resisted. Thus, fiction can serve as handmaiden to anthropological understanding.

In this context James Welch's acclaimed first novel, *Winter in the Blood*,[5] deserves special examination. Published in 1972, more than a generation later than McNickle's own first novel *The Surrounded* (1936),[6] which graphically portrayed the disintegrating effect of white civilization upon another Montana tribe, the Salish-Flatheads, *Winter in the Blood* brings that process up to date and then depicts a subtle reversal as the protagonist, in whom virtually all vestiges of Indian beliefs and customs appear to have been eradicated, reaches back toward prereservation culture and begins to reconstitute the tribal identity he personally had never possessed.[7]

At the outset of the novel, the narrator's situation is bleak. He has arrived at that nadir of nonidentity projected for the future in

McNickle's novel, which treated the first generation under reservation conditions. There the protagonist's family's tribal tie was initially compromised by interracial marriage. The household was dominated by the Spanish father who owned the ranch and battled with his fullblood wife and half-breed sons to keep them within the fold of white civilization. His experiment at cultural integration failed miserably, for his wife returned completely to Salish customs and his sons, whether acquiescent or rebellious, were destroyed by adversarial white officialdom. Meanwhile, fullblood Salish families retained some sense of community, but their most important religious ceremonies were banned, traditional means of livelihood precluded, and their children lost between cultures. They appeared well on the road to cultural extinction at the novel's end.

In *Winter in the Blood,* that same disintegrative process (which here involves a Montana Blackfeet family mistakenly located on the Fort Belknap reservation, composed mainly of Gros Ventres and Assiniboines) appears to be at the terminal stage. The allotment of individual parcels has broken the back of tribal community and the family unit is nucleated until no traditional supporting social structure of aunts, uncles, or cousins remains. There is more than a hint that the balance of socio-politico-economic power between the sexes has tilted so that women are domiant, for the narrator's mother owns the home ranch and the best reservation land of all belongs to Emily Short, a member of the tribal council. Such signs point to the greater erosion of roles and identity suffered by Indian males than females, a factor clearly indicated in McNickle's novel.

The narrator's predicament is further complicated because he mistakenly believes his tie to Indian traditions has been compromised by mixed tribal and racial blood, since he assumes his mother was produced by the union of his grandmother (he believes she is Gros Ventre but she is Blackfeet) and the halfbreed Doagie. His Blackfeet father, Half-Raise, denied the traditional male role as provider by hunting, often fantasizes about a manly trip to Glacier Park where he will defy the white man's abrogation of ancient hunting rights by illegally bagging an elk. But he knows he has no genius for intrigue and the game wardens will catch him. Bereft of community with his own family and tribe since the Blackfeet reservation is over 200 miles west of the Fort Belknap reservation, First Raise kicks ailing farm machinery into action and laughs with his boozing white clients in the bars of nearby Dodson. When his older son Mose is killed at age 14, the discouraged First Raise gradually abandons both his wife Teresa, who unceasingly complains about his vagabond Indian ways, and his younger son, the narrator, though a genuine bond of love exists between father and child.

As the novel opens, the 32-year-old narrator's loss of Indianness (and nearly everything else) appears a *fait accompli.* His senile maternal grandmother, now virtually speechless, totters on the brink of death. His father, now dead, drunkenly froze to death returning home during a blizzard. And his mother is preparing to marry the mercenary Lame Bull, who would out-white the Anglos in wringing profits from Teresa's rich lands and the hired hands. This is all the family the narrator possesses at the moment, except for the temporary presence of his Cree girlfriend, Agnes. As he returns home from his latest binge, he confesses total alienation from the land, human community, his family, and himself. His sympathy anesthetized, he identifies with neither Indian nor white culture: "I felt no hatred, no love, no guilt, no conscience, nothing but a distance that had grown through the years" (p. 4). This strange mental state arises from total suppression of empathy for all life forms, a denial of the configurating attitude underlying traditional Indian identity. Occupying a desensitized limbo between culturally different mindsets, the narrator seems ripe for assimilation into the configurating principle of Western culture, the objective and rationalistic mode of perception. He has no motive force to act, however.

The ensuing confrontation with his mother, Teresa, provides additional insight into the narrator's malaise. Ironically secure in her ownership of a Gros Ventres ranch, Teresa, who is unwittingly a fullblood Blackfeet, rejects Indian ways as heathenish and irresponsible. Her strong desire to assimilate already corrupted her first marriage, for she apparently put steady pressure on First Raise to practice the Anglo work ethic of diligent and punctual profit-making rather than the "shiftless" Indian pattern, which prizes visiting relatives and friends, participating in pow-wows and forty-niners, and simple "being" as opposed to competitive "becoming." Clearly, the narrator's father was an acculturated Indian, who learned white mechanical skills but retained allegiance to tribal culture though it is contravened considerably by marriage to an apparently mixed blood (white and Gros Ventre) woman. Here the distinction between acculturation and assimilation is rendered clearly by this ill-suited coupling. While John First Raise mysteriously resists the dominant culture's mindset until his untimely death, Teresa continues to see and judge the world from the white perspective.

A convert to Catholicism, Teresa makes common cause with a major force at work disintegrating Indian identity.[8] For example, she comically adopts Western magic, sprinkling holy water to protect the ranch house against lightning storms. A clear traitor to tribal religious beliefs, she "drank with the priest from Harlem, a round man with distant eyes, who refused to set foot on the reservation. He never buried Indians in the family graveyards; instead he made them come to him, to his church, his saints and his holy water, his feuding eyes" (p. 6). Churlish and unempathic, this partisan priest exemplifies the worst of the egoistic and rationalistic identity being forced on the Indians. At first, however, Teresa appears to be a resourceful survivor through her assimilationist approach. Possessing a fine and bitter repartee (she remarks to her suitor Lame Bull, "My son tells lies that would make a weasel think twice. He was cut from the same mold as you" (p. 12), she has dignity. She loves her decrepit fullblood mother and feels but mild contempt for her slovenly son, who inexplicably refuses the opportunities the white world offers to educated Indians like himself. In reality, Teresa is cut off from genuine community, either Indian or white, for she pursues the American dream of financial and social independence, which amounts to little more than alienation. Furthermore, an Indian who totally embraces white culture is likely to find himself or herself without intimate friends in either world. But unlike her son, she remains purposive, since she has maintained cognitive control of her world by abandoning one psycho-cultural system and adopting the competing one.

The situation of the narrator's girlfriend underscores the complexity of negotiating the gulfs between both tribes and races. Her Cree identity under double assault, she reads movie magazines, imagining she looks like Raquel Welch, an act tantamount to ethnic suicide. Meanwhile, as a tribal outsider she is scorned by the local reservation Gros Ventres. In this comedy of intertribal absurdities, the narrator's chair-ridden grandmother, still carrying on ancient Blackfeet grudges in her mind, plots ways to slit Agnes' Cree throat. Such is Welch's sardonic, but still loving, portrait of the tribal family crumbling under the combined pressures of white domination and lingering intertribal hostilities.

But even as the narrator returns momentarily to his bizarre

family circle, notes of resistance to European-derived mentality are struck, primarily in images of the natural world—birds, animals, and streams, which still survive the onslaught of the whiteman. They are living proof that "civilization" is not irresistable. More than symbols of nonassimilation, they convey messages of wisdom from the sacred realm of nature, the source of tribal wisdom itself. Witness the remarkable Milk River, which remains impervious to either the whiteman's careless pollution from a sugar beet factory (now defunct for seven years) or his guilty but fumbling attempts to rehabilitate it by planting foreign species to replace the presumably extinct native trout. In a brilliant image we see symbolized one strategy of the native mindset in resisting foreign traits: "the river ignored the fish and the fish ignored the river" (p. 9). This process exactly fits Spindler's description of adopting "conflicting elements under duress and keeping them rigidly segmented from the Indian cognitive world." And when the narrator angles in this emblematic stream, the creatures of nature speak to reawaken his intuitive consciousness: "A magpie squawked from deep in the woods on the other side of the river" (p. 10). Later, as he thumbs through an old issue of *Sports Afield*, his eyes fall upon an advertisement for "a fishing lure that called to fish in their own language.... Maybe that was the secret" (p. 16), he reflects. Unbeknownst to himself, he has already begun on the path toward recapturing the Indian mind. But his journey is beset with many obstacles that represent assimilative forces at work negating the values, lifeways, and spirit of the tribal world.

In Teresa's new husband Lame Bull,[9] he encounters an Indian whose personal predilection for insensitivity to the natural life, which would have been suppressed by tribal culture, has fully blossomed. It is the cornerstone upon which the whiteman's technological civilization is constructed. In the fierce quest for profit, the once-impoverished Lame Bull no longer considers the rights of all other species to share in nature's bounty. As the first crop is brought in, "Lame Bull mows alfalfa, snakes, bluejoint, baby rabbits, tangles of barbed wire" (p. 29). On the other hand, the hired hand for haying, Raymond Long Knife, once a champion cowboy, is an amusing caricature of undiscriminating cultural resistance that fails to recognize legitimate work and thereby lowers already diminished self-esteem another notch. He has learned "to give the illusion of work even to the point of sweating as soon as he puts his gloves on, while doing very little" (p. 30). But the women, perversely, seem to thrive as masculinity ebbs. Raymond's mother Belva outcowboys the males of her family, riding long hours, wrestling calves, castrating them, and then pointedly "eating the roasted balls" while she stares down the abashed men. As these dramatic images indicate, the Indian male ego has been devastated by the fact of conquest, though it may still resist adopting white behavior.

For the narrator, his own repugnance to total capitulation of Indian identity is lodged within memories of the past. There, a single fragment of poetry is constituted by his grandmother's brief tribal glory as the newly married third wife of the Blackfeet chief Standing Bear. Though she bore him no child before he was killed in a desperate raid on the Gros Ventres for food and she then endured complete ostracism for bringing the bad luck of the chief's death (her arrival in the tribe coincided with invasion of Blackfeet territory by white soldiers), the grandmother nonetheless imprints in the narrator's mind the undying Indian spirit of oneness with the natural world and the sense of living beauty. The other sustaining memory, that of his beloved brother Mose, for whose death he assumes overwhelming responsibility, recalls a near idyllic period in his own life when the boys rode free out on the land of their ancestors. Unfortunately the forces of assimilation were already effectually at work. We later find that the unwitting adoption of arrogant white attitudes towards animals tragically precipitates Mose's death when the two brothers, in an adolescent attempt to impress their father, escalate the natural schedule of bringing the cattle in from the grazing range. They haze the animals callously, rushing them down to the ranch, and Mose is killed in retribution. From then on, the emotionally frozen brother remains a "servant to the memory of death" (p. 45), for he has no traditional extended family to help him deal with such a devastating crisis. Trapped in the past, he remains poised between the potentially regenerative memory of his grandmother's past and the paralytic memory of his own assimilative present. He appears curiously like the individual Spindler described, unable to relate to either cognitive system, unable to act at all.[10]

The middle part of the novel sets into active motion these countervailing destructive and redemptive forces. The narrator returns to town, ostensibly searching for Agnes, who made off with his gun and electric razor (symbols of white masculinity), so he can make her suffer. Welch provides a richly comic but hurtful inventory of

other forces working to disintegrate the Indian psyche. Discovering
that Agnes has discarded him for a white man who has money and a
"big-assed Buick," the narrator stupidly helps Agnes' brother rob her
new lover. Then the entire town seems turned against him. It is full of
"stalking whitemen." But the Indians, drunk at Gable's bar, are no
bargains either. They have nothing left to do but pimp for their sisters,
compete against their red brothers for white dollars, and besot
themselves. There is no trace of racism, however, in Welch's treatment
of this intercultural circus, no animosity towards whites. Both races
perform ritualistically in a drama whose roles are clear but whose
intercultural significance is totally obscure to all participants.

Returning to the ranch, the narrator decides to visit an old
neighbor, once a confidant of First Raise, the now blind Yellow Calf.
As the only articulate survivor of the Indian past, he initially serves as
a measure of the young man's distance from the native mindset.
Yellow Calf's social isolation makes no sense to the narrator who sees
solely through white perspectives. He banters the old man, in a
smartassed fashion, telling him "there's something wrong with you.
No man should live alone" (p. 78). Yellow Calf's response ("who's
alone?") indicts the great reductionism of white vision, for he is
surrounded by living, empathic, communicating creatures. In an
astonishing reversal of the Western view of nature's hierarchy, the old
Blackfeet opines that men are the last to understand the true nature of
things. The deer recognize full well that the world has been turned
cockeyed by the advent of the exploitive, destructive, and partisan-
spirited whiteman. Though the narrator tries to trip up Yellow Calf
by clever refutations ("to a deer one year is as good as the next"), the old
man decisively defends the wisdom of our animal relatives. The
narrator leaves bemused, bearing Yellow Calf's mysterious message
to Teresa that "I am living to the best of my ability" (p. 80). Meanwhile,
the old man stands listening absorbedly to two magpies argue,
distilling the gist of the debate.

Clearly the narrator has little inkling why he is not living to the
best of his ability, but Yellow Calf has cracked ajar the door into tribal
consciousness. Nonetheless, he reenters the crazy, drunken world of
barrooms and of promiscuous and uncaring sex. Again we see
concretely some mechanisms by which the white world has destroyed
the unity of tribal spirit and the sense of belonging. We get a brief case
history of Malvina, who "trained for two years at Haskell, learning

how to squiggle while some big-nuts shot his mouth off, and never even worked the first day" (p. 90).[11] Sexual, not secretarial, skills were all her prospective employers thought Indian women were fit for. Such is the ironic fate of cultural sycophants who so hastily shed Indian identity. Balanced against Malvina is the paranoiac airplane man, a white embezzler pursued by the feds. He epitomizes the astounding reductionism to which the dominant culture subjects its own natives; verily, the pursuit of money is the only legitimate (and illegitimate) occupation. In all this kaleidoscopic chaos of cultural miscegenation, the narrator pursues Agnes, his only living tie with the warmth of human feeling. He finally realizes he actually *wants* to do something. "I wanted to follow her . . . I wanted to be with her, but I didn't move" (p. 112). Still paralyzed by indecision, he lets slip the opportunity; but feeling now begins to return more strongly, his heart strangely opened by the recent visit to the anachronistic old man who believes that the world and all its creatures are still alive.

Off guard, his repressed memory shoots back to the traumatic moment leading to Mose's death when the boys are hazing the herd headlong down the mountain, cursing the cattle and vowing to carry a gun next time to "blast" the playful coyote pups they see. He now glimpses that this terrible attitude towards the Great Spirit's creatures, our true relatives, precipitated Mose's death. He catches up with Agnes finally and admits to a love or lust for her, seeing in her eyes "the promise of warm things, of a spirit that went beyond her miserable life of drinking and screwing and men like me" (p. 125).[12] Unfortunately, his lights are treacherously punched out at that moment. When he regains consciousness outside the bar, he is taken by Marlene, a compassionate but lost whore who hopes to restore some link with life by sexual promiscuity. But after making love, in a last burst of white objectivist mentality, the narrator leaps astride Marlene's naked belly and rides her into frustrated submission. While she struggles tremendously to free herself, her conqueror stares "at the sobbing woman with the same lack of emotion, the same curiosity, as though (he) were watching a bug floating motionless down an irrigation ditch, not yet dead but having decided upon death" (p. 138). When he slides off finally, he falls once more into the sleep of complete anesthesia, the longed for boon of self-annihilation, since he really has no stomach for the machismo expected of white he-men.

The climactic scene marks his turning away from the path of

assimilation and toward his true heritage. Driven back home by a professor and his family, he feels compassion for the pretty but consumptive daughter, later eating out of loyalty the bitter apple she presents him, a scene which delightfully parodies by inversion the Garden of Eden myth. He recalls the hawk he once pridefully shot from the sky, a wanton killing, now sorrowfully remembering its tongue, which an Indian would regard as showing its true nature— "personal, private, even human." He washes off the dirt—"the invisible kind that coats a man who has been to town"—ironically baptizing himself out of white culture and further into his tribal heritage. Egotism waning, breadth of vision returns. He observes the farm animals and now appreciates their genuine participation in the real world. His attentiveness is reciprocated, for "they all watched him with interest" (p. 152).

Recognizing that man is bound to all creatures with necessary if fragile ties, he finally admits the real reason for Mose's death, disrespect for animals: "We shouldn't have run them, I thought, it wasn't good for them" (p. 159). He is then able to relive the entire scenario, as the boys, having miscalulated the waning daylight, frantically push the cattle downhill; "we had them racing full tilt down the hill into the valley, both of us swearing and swatting their behinds with the ends of our ropes" (p. 161). Acceptance of that heavy responsibility prepares him for a truly epiphanous insight into his real place in the world.

Upon his arrival home, he realizes his old Blackfoot grandmother has died; the house is deserted. Her death unccountably moves him to visit Yellow Calf again, this time carrying a bottle of wine out of respect for the old man. As he rides Old Bird, he is able after twenty years to forgive the old horse his part in the tragedy of Mose's death, recognizing the cowpony simply reacted as he was trained, bolting after the runaway calf, causing Mose to pursue them out on the highway to his death. Through true empathy to an animal relative, the narrator understands how Old Bird *feels* about being broken white-man's style, cruelly against his will and nature. Only the threat of death made him give in to his conqueror, much as some Indians have to theirs. The true culprit here is brutality of spirit, the Western belief that man can abrogate with impunity the rights the Great Spirit has given to all other living beings.

At Yellow Calf's cabin, assisted by deepening empathy and thirst to learn about his native origins, the narrator gently probes into the ancient Indian's recollections about the departed grandmother and the unfortunate saga of Standing Bear's band of Blackfeet. An emergent intuition now directs his questions toward the mystery of his family's sources. When he cannot quite accept the validity of the people banishing his grandmother for bringing bad luck, Yellow Calf admonishes him to stretch his ethnic imagination: "You must understand the thinking" (p. 175). And while he can't grasp what he still regards as an arcane Blackfeet notion of medicine at work, he acknowledges that it was, as Yellow Calf says, "the way things were." This capitulation to the tribal mind leads to an inimitably Indian epiphany where the excretory and the sacred unite. Old Bird suddenly farts and it comes to him "as though it were riding one moment of the gusting wind as though Bird had had it in him all the time and has passed it to me in that instance of corruption" (p. 179). The conveyance of animal wisdom can be passing strange. In the transcendence of holistic vision, the narrator perceives his entire history. He *sees* how his ostracized grandmother was provided for by the youthful hunter, Yellow Calf, who later actually fathered Teresa. He *sees* how, out of respect for the grandmother's standing as the widow of the renowned Standing Bear, Yellow Calf would carry on secretively the twenty-five year long affair. In this marvelously affecting scene, both men appreciate the humorous paradox by which the long lost grandfather is revealed. They share a wonderful moment of deepest unity "in the presence of ghosts, in the wind that called forth the muttering teepees, the blowing snow, the white air of horses' nostrils" (p. 179). Time, especially the interval containing the whiteman's conquest, is obliterated and the narrator is restored in spirit to his old Blackfoot heritage. As he rides away, he now understands why Yellow Calf has earlier withheld from him that crucial information and why he too will never tell his mother of her completely Indian origins until her spirit is likewise prepared to make that fact transcendently meaningful. He knows that the touchstone of the truth, "the feeling of event," resides in the holistic wisdom of the blood which unites us to all living beings. That is the configurating principle of the Indian mind. Henceforth, so long as that spirit remains dominant, the narrator will be truly free of cultural oppression. In the future he can freely acculturate any aspect of white culture he chooses so long as it can be fitted into the tribal mindset.

Freed from the stasis of nonidentity, the narrator can now confront the remaining obstacle in his life, guilt over his complicity in Mose's death and his alienation from First Raise. They were, after all, the only two people he ever loved in his old life. Returning to the ranch, he is accosted by Ferdinand Horn and his wife, two apple Indians (red on the outside, white on the inside). Ferdinand can't refrain from "measuring the field," trying to calculate how many bales it produces, while his wife probes spitefully into the narrator's love life. But her malicious queries about Agnes touch a newly sensitized spot. "It was a stab in the heart" he acknowledges. He goes on toward the corral, only to discover the wild-eyed cow sinking fatally into the slough. Responding with hatred (he remembers "the image of catastrophe, the same hateful eye . . . the wild-eyed spinster" who caused Mose's death),[13] he tries to ignore her. But he can no longer pretend animals are disenfranchised puppets of man. He forces himself through the mud hobbling on the leg injured during Mose's accident, stupidly puts a loop around the cow's neck (rather than her horns), and urges Old Bird to haul her out. Aware of his foolish risk, from the whiteman's egocentric perspective, he curses the horse, the Horns, Lame Bull, damned Indians, and "this greedy, stupid country." But it is his last vomiting forth of the white cognitive world. The desperate effort succeeds, though Old Bird dies in the final tug. But when the dying horse begins to topple backwards on the narrator, the weight of the old cow restrains the fall, protecting his life. That is the saving balance provided by respecting other animals.

As he later attends his grandmother's funeral, now reconciled to his past and therefore his future, the narrator is in tune with the entire earth, knowing that the newly fallen rain will be "good for fishing." Wearing First Raise's suit, which is embellished by his father's silk tie "with a picture of two mallards flying over an island of cattails," he is prepared to wish the old fullblood lady well in her trip to the spirit world. The only real Indian at the ceremony, he throws her medicine pouch into the grave. Against the backdrop of Lame Bull's wonderfully inept funeral oration, the narrator decides to set his world aright. First he will see if Agnes will really marry him. Then there is that bum knee to have operated on. It is a real, if tentative, start. For he finally possesses an identity capable of affirming the worth of his people, himself, and all the living world. While he still knows precious little of everyday Blackfeet life, he has recaptured its configurating principle. He has retribalized himself against all odds, himself proof that assimilation is not inevitable.[14]

Since the novel concludes here,[15] we are left pondering the narrator's prospects. Can he, for example, reshape his part in the chaos of reservation life so that the old Blackfeet love for all creation will have positive embodiment? It is one thing to possess the spirit of tribalism, another to live by its principles in modern times. One hopes for further visits with Yellow Calf, perhaps in the company of Agnes and other members of the narrator's generation who are tired of acculturated and miserable lives. Clearly, the white world's insistence upon total assimilation has a purely negative influence upon the Indian people. It aims only at cultural genocide, the extinction of Indian identity; but it has no plans to adopt tribal members into the mainstream national culture. Paradoxically, white bigotry and greed have been main conservators of Indianness.[16]

Although *Winter in the Blood* is a work of the imagination, its fictive truth considerably extends our historical and anthropological understanding. In the lives of its people, we not only watch the processes of assimilation and acculturation at work, but also we are privy to the specific mechanics of capitulation or resistance as individual characters make their ways through the no-man's land of intercultural warfare. Because the abstract has been made flesh, we can see why it is possible that some Indians can successfully resist the "civilized" mindset and culture against absolutely overwhelming odds. This work of imaginative literature, then, need not accept the role as handmaiden to scientific study of ethnic persistence. Rather, it is itself mistress to that higher truth towards which all human inquiry ultimately aims.

Notes

[1]See D'Arcy McNickle, *Native American Tribalism: Indian Survivals and Renewals* (New York: Oxford University Press, 1973), pp. 4-5.

[2]A. Irving Hallowell, "Ojibwa Personality and Acculturation," in *Acculturation in the Americas*, Sol Tax, ed., Selected Papers of the XXIX International Congress of Americanists, Vol. 2, 1925, p. 110. See also Hallowell's *Culture and Experience* (Philadelphia: University of Pennsylvania Press, 1955) and his fine essay on Indian influences, "The Impact of the American Indian on American Culture," *American Anthropologist*, 59 (1957), 201-17.

[3]George D. Spindler, "Psychocultural Adaptation" in *The Study of Personality: An Interdisciplinary Appraisal*, E. Norbeck et al., eds. (New York: Holt, Rinehart, and Winston, 1968), p. 340.

[4]*Native American Tribalism*, p. 10.

[5]All references will be to the Harper & Row Bantam edition first printed in 1974.

[6]Now available in the 1978 edition by the University of New Mexico Press.

[7]A good beginning for critical commentary on *Winter in the Blood* is the special symposium issue of *American Indian Quarterly*, Vol. 4, No. 2 (May 1978). See also Alan R. Velie's chapter on Welch in *Four American Indian Literary Masters* (Norman: University of Oklahoma, 1982), pp. 91-103.

[8]McNickle's *The Surrounded* powerfully indicts Catholicism as the most destructive agent against traditional Salish culture.

[9]In Ruoff's article appearing in the symposium issue of *AIQ*, she indicates Lame Bull is "the name of the novelist's Gros Ventre grandfather, James Smith O'Bryan." Lame Bull was also a noted Piegan chief, according to John C. Ewers, *The Blackfeet: Raiders on the Northwestern Plains* (Norman: University of Oklahoma, 1958), pp. 218, 222-23.

[10]In *House Made of Dawn* (New York: New American Library, 1969), N. Scott Momaday punningly designates his inept Indian protagonist Able.

[11]Again, Welch's drawing from personal experience is evident in even brief characterizations. See Ronald McFarland, "An Interview with James Welch," in this edition. Welch's Gros Ventre mother went to Haskell and "learned secretarial skills." But she, unlike Malvina, makes a success of it.

[12]Agnes' spirit indicates the pressure, however suppressed, of the tribal world.

[13]It is not clear that this is the same cow as the wild-eyed spinster who precipitated Mose's death, since she would have to be several years past 20. That's unlikely, but the present cow is sufficiently similar to do even if she is not the original.

[14]Vine Deloria, Jr. in several books, especially *We Talk, You Listen*, argues that the tide of assimilation has reversed nationwide. Now even white people are inevitably, if slowly, becoming tribalized.

Mystery and Mock Intrigue in James Welch's *Winter in the Blood*

Robert Gish

Much of the tragicomic effect of James Welch's masterful novel, *Winter in the Blood* (1974), depends on the elements of mystery and mock intrigue and their thematic and structural interplay.[1] Although mystery and mock intrigue are identifiable as distinct and separate elements throughout the novel, they are nevertheless organically related, not only to each other but to the central metaphor of the book and all of its accompanying imagery—the pervasive notion of "winter in the blood."

Precisely because Welch's book is so organic, mystery and mock intrigue are cornerstones in his construction of point of view and method of narration; in the rendering of character—especially that of the nameless narrator; in advancing the plot; in the sense of setting and the atmosphere of "Big Sky" Montana; and in overall theme and imagery—the anatomy of the language itself.

Without attempting an exhaustive analysis of the ways in which all of these aspects of *Winter in the Blood* relate to each other, I seek merely to illustrate partially how mystery and mock intrigue work together in the composition of this fascinating novel. I do not mean to suggest that such a consideration is the only way to approach the novel. Welch's artistry is too richly complex for that. But a consideration of mystery and mock intrigue provides a way of synthesizing views which see the novel as either tragic or comic; either a native American or a non-ethnic book; either a modern psychological novel or a Western; either regional or universal; either one thing or the other.

Neither do I mean by the use of the terms "mystery" and "mock intrigue" that *Winter in the Blood* is limited to being a full-fledged Mystery novel; nor that it is an open-throttled, no-holds-barred parody of the Spy novel or the novel of Intrigue. Mystery and mock intrigue are intended more broadly than that for purposes of the present discussion. In such a context, *Winter in the Blood* is viewed as only a partial parody of the Spy novel. Simultaneously, *Winter in the Blood* may be read as having certain characteristics (certainly not all) of the Mystery or Detective novel. There are, to be sure, many minor "crimes" and at least two major mysterious deaths to solve (call them "murders," or, more specifically, suicide and manslaughter?) This is to say that in terms of literary genre and mode, *Winter in the Blood* is no one, single thing. It is a realistic novel, a surrealist poem, an absurdist drama, a picaresque, mock-epic adventure, a sociological satire on American Indian and non-Indian relations, a modern, "adult" Western—in short, *Winter in the Blood* defies easy classification. Because of its kaleidoscopic nature, the novel invites broad definitions and merged definitions. And that is why mystery and mock intrigue are intended broadly here.

All three traditional definitions of mystery apply: (1) anything that arouses curiosity because it is unexplained, inexplicable, or secret; (2) the quality of being inexplicable or secret; and (3) a piece of fiction dealing with a puzzling crime. Intrigue may be defined as (1) a covert or underhand scheme; (2) the use of such schemes or to engage in them; (3) a clandestine love affair; (4) suspense and mystery. Mock intrigue then, is, as might be expected, the mocking of intrigue and its associated narrative conventions for humorous and satirical ends—or even, as in the case of *Winter in the Blood*, the ends of tragedy and pathos.[2]

There is, admittedly, a certain redundancy in the use of the two terms together insofar as "mystery" suggests intrigue, and "intrigue" in turn suggests "mystery." This redundancy is compounded in that the interplay of these elements in the novel first expand and then contract—are, in terms of fictive spatial form, expansive and reflexive. In the broadest architectonic terms I equate "mystery" with the more serious, profoundly tragic ideas and events and feelings (or in this instance, lack of feelings) which cluster around the narrator and his center of consciousness (benumbed and awakened, "distanced" and "immediate"; that is, the "blood consciousness," as it were, that comes from within the narrator and is associated with the book's title and controlling metaphor, and which is evoked in its numerous "objective correlatives," to call upon T. S. Eliot's terminology). Also in an architectonic context, I equate mock intrigue with the more comic, often blackly comic and absurdist, satirical aspects of the narrator—his life, his perceptions, and, behind him, Welch's perceptions. Mock intrigue is also extended to those people, ideas, and events which affect and are effected by the narrator—experiences which are never truly assimilated by him, never puzzled out—or if they are understood, they are taken as nothing much more than trifles.

Seen this way, the scheme of the book is such that the dominant "mystery" includes the death of the narrator's brother, Mose; the death of the narrator's father, First Raise; the true identity of Yellow Calf and his relationship with the narrator's grandmother, and the larger genealogy of the Blackfeet peoples; the true nature of the narrator's injury—just how he came to suffer from his "wounded knee" and what caused his initial and ostensibly terminally benumbed, winterized mental and emotional state. Certainly the separate "mysteries" of all these major facets of the novel are intricately interrelated once they are "figured out" by the narrator and dramatized and explained for the reader who is working just as hard as the narrator throughout the book—but by means of ratiocination and inference more so than memory (although that is also a factor) —to find out just what is happening in the narrator's present and what went on in his past. Past and present converge variously throughout the novel, but most powerfully after the narrator's grandmother dies and he is once again digging a grave. At that point the narrator's repressed trauma over the death of Mose (and by extension, of First Raise) is not only understood but felt—with all the collision force of the ill-fated, careening automobile striking Mose and his horse, as if in some kind of "explosive" movie of the mind. Architectonically this is accomplished by means of Welch's skillful use of suspense, of foreshadowing and flashbacks, of expanding and reflexive imagery and symbolism.

In comparison to the actual experience of reading the novel, of figuring things out, attempting to methodically explain Welch's utilization of suspenseful and dynamic imagery is a paltry enterprise. The novel is so tightly and subtly stitched, so supremely coherent and unified in spite of the ultimately superficial, always deceptive confusion,

that an explanation of one element under the heading of "mystery"
soon leads to another sub-heading and eventually to another major
heading of "mock intrigue." This is a reminder that a consideration of
mystery, as I have outlined its association with the tragic aspects of the
book, soon turns to a consideration of mock intrigue.

◆

The idea of the narrator's "wounded knee," as a symbol or
objective correlative of both his physical and psychic injury sustained
when he is thrown from Bird (that great white horse) at the scene of his
brother's death on a wintry Montana highway, is one such instance of
Welch's mastery at merging mystery and mock intrigue. The narrator's
numb but aching knee is simultaneously a tragicomic implied pun, a
joke, played on both the narrator and the audience, on both the
processes of history and fiction, by Welch's sense of life. There are
many such merged, ironic instances, joinings of mystery and mock
intrigue (often they are instances of dramatic irony), where Welch
allows the reader significant clues which add another whole dimension
of detective role-playing by the reader, beyond fiction and into the
even more baffling sequence of cause and effect called history.

    The entire interpolated, seemingly digressive history of Yellow
Calf and grandmother and the winter he spent looking after her when
she was abandoned by the Blackfeet tribe; his own revealed identity as
a Blackfeet rather than a Gros Ventre, is another episode suggestive of
the tragic mysteries, the comic intrigues of both fiction and history,
invented and real, experienced and told. Another example of how
Welch merges mystery with mock intrigue is in his treatment of the
narrator's Cree girlfriend, her role as antagonist to grandmother, her
absconding with the narrator's ironically personal but valueless
possessions of razor and gun, and her escape which provides the
overall framework for the journey (actually several journeys) which
the narrator must take to find her. As a runaway, pictured at one point
with green, creme-de-menthe coated teeth, at once the potential object
of the narrator's love and of grandmother's hate and plotted
assassination, Agnes is a comprehensive vehicle for Welch's nicely
confused (confused but controlled) portrayal of a simultaneously
meaningless and meaningful love.

If the search for Agnes provides the framework for the characters and events which contribute to the mock intrigue of the novel, the narrator's relationships with other characters give the novel's mock intrigue its substance. Good-natured and self-serving Lame Bull and moaning Teresa; Ferdinand Horn and his bespectacled, inquiring wife; flashy cowboy Ray Long Knife and Belva, his hungry mother; Teresa and her clandestine relationship with Father Kitteredge, the priest in Harlem, as well as her relationship with her sons, Mose and the narrator, her first husband, First Raise, and with her reputed father, the half-breed drifter, Doagie—all of these intrigues which take as their locale the Earthboy ranch, provide one important nodality.

The highway between the towns with their endless string of bars, and the towns themselves, provide two other nodalities which give substance to the mock intrigue in the novel. The women which the narrator meets on the road to his discoveries and rememberings as he sallies forth, a pathetic, drunken and debilitated picaro, up and down the valley from the Earthboy ranch and his reservation home—from Dodson to Malta to Harlem to Havre and back again—provide even more substance to his "quest" for Agnes. The women include the bosomy barmaid in Malta; the tatooed mother, Malvina, in Harlem; and the wanton Marlene, in Havre. Laced throughout the narrator's search for Agnes; his pursuit by her brother, Dougie (easily and significantly confused by the reader with Teresa's alleged father and the narrator's reputed grandfather, Doagie); and including the narrator's promiscuous sexual escapades, is his utterly confusing and anti-climatic involvement with the fugitive from New York, the "airplane man" whose grand plan for getaway across the border into Canada, in, of all things, a Ford Falcon, instigates some of the most hilarious and nonsensical scenes in the novel.

It is admittedly dangerous to reduce a novel as complex as *Winter in the Blood* to two categories of mystery on the one hand and mock intrigue on the other—with a buffer zone of sorts resting in between where the two elements overlap. Nevertheless, having proposed this scheme and these categories, some more specific analysis is in order. For present purposes, that analysis is limited to the characters of Mose and the "airplane man" and their respective contributions to the mystery and mock intrigue, the tragedy and comedy of the book.

The reader does not discover what really happened to Mose, does not find out the details of his death, until the end of part three, 163 pages into the 199-page novel. The reader is aware from the beginning of the novel that Mose is dead and so is his father, First Raise. The reader has clues concerning the way in which Mose died; but for all practical purposes Mose's death is a mystery. And because the narrator has repressed the anguish of his brother's death, the "mystery" of it extends to the narrator. Through Welch's manipulations, the book builds on its most tragic level to the dramatic reenactment of that death—so that both the narrator and the reader actually "see" the accident again (in the case of the narrator), and for the first time (in the case of the reader):

> I couldn't have seen it—we were still moving in the opposite direction, the tears, the dark and wind in my eyes—the movie exploded whitely in my brain, and I saw the futile lurch of the car as the brake lights popped, the horse's shoulder caving before the fender, the horse spinning so that its rear end smashed into the door, the smaller figure flying slowly over the top of the car to land with the hush of a stuffed doll.
>
> The calf stopped at the sound of collision. Bird jolted down the slope of the shoulder and I tumbled from his back, down into the dark weeds I felt my knee strike something hard, a rock maybe, or a culvert, then the numbness. (p. 163)

For the narrator, this reenactment, this dredged-up recollection is a psychological and emotional catharsis which seems to amount to a degree of improvement, ironically, in his zombie-like condition, a thawing out of his metaphorical "winterized" sense of death. The physical death had been Mose's; but the complementary spiritual death was the narrator's—both deaths occasioned when the anonymous, drunken driver collided with Mose and his horse. At the same moment in the novel, the cause of the narrator's injured knee, and its literal and figurative significance also becomes clear. He too had suffered a collision, with either a rock or a culvert, when he sailed off of Bird (paralleling Mose's flight) and smashed his leg. But not everything is known, even yet. Mysteries still remain. Who was the driver? Was his bad breath caused by alcohol? What did the narrator's knee hit, exactly? Even upon this final revelation, questions linger behind the answers. Inference suffices rather than certainty.

Images of explosion and collision cluster around the revelation of the circumstances of Mose's death, and serve by way of widening referents to supplement the solution of the mystery of why the narrator is so disoriented, so dazed, so punchy. All of the fists in the face: Lame Bull's punching of Raymond Long Knife; Dougie's slugging of the narrator; and all of the cars in the book, and their motion—the Ford Falcon; the "big smooth-riding Oldsmobile" in which the narrator hitches a ride back home from Havre; the "black pickup" which roars past him with Teresa and Lame Bull inside; the dark-green Hudson of Ferdinand and Mrs. Horn—all of the collision and car imagery builds to and recedes from the moment and the memory of Mose's death. Similarly, the pervasive imagery of winter, of literal and figurative coldness, and the persistent animal imagery reinforce the cause-and-effect mystery behind Mose's death. But all of the imagery which creates and unravels the mysteries surrounding Mose's death only serves to underscore the biggest mystery of all: "Why did Mose have to die," "Why Mose?" "Why death?"

Welch, the narrator, and the reader are all left with that imponderable, dramatized yet again at the graveside of grandmother— and in the final whinnying of the other horses for Bird.

For the narrator, First Raise's death is only superficially more understandable than Mose's death. And, as with Mose's death, it is not clear at the beginning of the novel that the death of First Raise—found frozen in a barrow pit across from the Earthboy place—is an imagistic repetition of the cold weather when the narrator and Mose drove First Raise's cattle across that fateful highway. And it is not at all clear at the start that First Raise's death is directly linked to the death of Mose. Grandmother's grave, Mose's grave, First Raise's grave are all part of the same mystery. Significantly, the narrator remembers Mose's death, as fully as he is capable, in the family cemetery plot. It is not initially obvious that First Raise's death was caused as much by guilt and grief as it was by drink and exposure. We learn that it is First Raise who makes the request for the cattle drive, arranges it and sends the boys off, ironically, with love and a good breakfast—as the pathos of the story would have it. It is First Raise who primes that particular mystery.

Teresa insists that it was an anonymous "they" who found First Raise alongside the road. The narrator remembers riding the highways looking in the barrow pits and thinks that "we," that the family and not "they," found First Raise's frozen body. And as the confusion about so many things multiplies (including the mystery and the mock intrigue of whether First Raise or Teresa or somebody else killed Amos), the narrator's unreliablility grows. Moreover, this unreliability is in itself mysterious.

In addition to being connected to the tragic mystery of Mose's death, First Raise is connected to the mystery of the narrator's ancestry and identity. It is First Raise who takes the narrator when still a child to visit Yellow Calf one winter. This detail is remembered only after the narrator's realization that Yellow Calf is his grandfather; that he is Teresa's father—not the half-white drifter, Doagie. (The confusion of Doagie's name with Dougie; of Raymond Long Knife's name with the Long-knife soldiers; of Marlene with Malvina; of Yellow Calf with his outrageous nickname of Batman; of the New Yorker's alias, "airplane man"—all of the multiple and duplicate names serve likewise to heighten the confusion.)

As a kind of mock-epic, senile, "blind-seer," Yellow Calf knows the answers to many mysteries—those of ancestry learned through his own experiences as a hunter and provider for grandmother during that one particular hard, historical, loving winter; and he knows those answers learned from the deer and his own internalized, visionary secrets. During his visits with Yellow Calf the narrator must tease out some of the answers to those mysteries. Yellow Calf is assuredly an instance of mock intrigue and comedy. But the mysteries to which he knows the answers, and which First Raise realizes much before the narrator does, play heavily on the narrator's own alienation and his mystery of identity. Until such mysteries are answered, the faces of First Raise, of the drifter, Doagie, of Yellow Calf, of the New York fugitive, and even of the narrator himself including his disputed age, will remain confused.

That confusion is reinforced by the virtually ancient ages of Bird and the spinster cow. The deliberate ambiguities of whether or not the spinster cow the narrator attempts to save at the end of the novel is indeed the same animal which balked at the time of Mose's accident, and of Bird's age and implied death, also heighten the mysteries of just who the narrator was and who he is now.

◆

The biggest comic mock intrigue which contributes to the deliberate confusion of the novel surrounds the identity and motivation of the man from New York, the so-called "airplane man" who is on the lam and in Montana presumably to make a getaway across the border into Canada. The narrator's initial and recurrent meetings with the New York fugitive provide a major focus for the element of mock intrigue. The airplane man is even more anonymous than the narrator and although less tragically mysterious, he is nevertheless just as comically intriguing.

Their first meeting comes in Malta, in the ironic squalor of the Pomp Room. That meeting begins on a ludicrous note of irony and ambiguity which establishes the terms for all their future dealings. The airplane man, although running away from his past life, attempts to prove to the narrator that he is indeed from New York—and shows him his credit cards to "prove" it. He is dressed in khaki and reminds the narrator significantly of the lion hunters (known intimately not from life but from the printed page as McLeod and Henderson) whom he has read about in the *Sports Afield* story which works as an interpolated tale in the opening pages of the novel and as an expansive image throughout. That hunt went around in circles—and so will the narrator's "hunt" for the airplane man's identity and past as the narrator circles his way between towns and the ranch looking for Agnes and his possessions. First Raise's perpetually planned hunt in Glacier National Park is another echo of similar futility.

The airplane man announces that he was at one time a rich man, and that he had a wife and two daughters. But his purpose is to solve the problems that the narrator does not remember having. Despite his avowal to help the narrator with his problems, the New Yorker continues to talk about his own life—continues to offer clues as to who he is and why he is in Montana and at the moment talking to someone he doesn't even know. For a presumed fugitive he is strangely talkative. He garrulously tells the narrator that he was on his way to the Middle East, ready to board a plane, when he tore up his tickets in front of "her," picked up his fishing gear and drove away. Who "she" is, the narrator and the reader can only guess—for the airplane man assumes, again ironically, thanks to Welch, that the narrator and the reader know more than we do. Each spoken and implied detail leads circuitously to add to the mock intrigue, the humor of the situation as event and dialog.

After an argument about catching fish where none are to be caught, the argument becomes even more bizarre with confusions about Minnesota and the promise of the best steak in—of all the crazy places—Kalamazoo, if they don't catch any fish. There is more than one kind of fishing expedition going on here. And the hunting and fishing imagery all reinforce the intrigue. The reader, and even the narrator, soon realize that there is an absurdity present that goes beyond the burblings of two ordinary drunks.

To heighten the zaniness of the intrigue, two men dressed in suits that smell of wet wool come into the bar (more like rain-drenched sheepherders than special agents). They move "down the bar like cows on slick ice" (p. 57), an inherently comic image, but one that also conjures up the scene of Mose's death. The bartender "stalks" them down the other side of the bar on a miniature "tailing" mission of his own. The two men are ostensibly followed by the airplane man. Confusion increases when a fish called "gold eyes" is introduced into the conversation and the two men in suits are turned to as referees in the dispute (the unlikeliest of roles)—while the barmaid blows smoke rings to obfuscate things visually with the smoke and its symbolic circles—from a cigarette, a source, undiscovered by the narrator.

As pursued and pursuers disagree about whether or not local fishing waters are clear or muddy, (another symbolic obfuscation), the discussion continues on its own way of comic misunderstandings. And when the airplane man thinks that he recognizes the barmaid from times either in Bismarck, Minneapolis, Chicago, Seattle, or San Francisco—from one end of the country to the other—the inane befuddlement compounds itself in a string of totally "off the wall" non-sequiturs about roses and morning glories and cats and birth-marks. While the airplane man tries to pin down his identification, not of himself this time, but of the barmaid, she attempts to explain to the narrator why she is only partially recognizable to the airplane man:

> 'He used to pay me. That's why I hated it. He used to pay me a dollar to dance for him.' She laughed. 'It was such fun, twirling around the room, faster and faster until I must have been a blur. That's why he forgets my face.' (p. 59)

What did she hate? Their relationship? She says, contradictorily, that she thought the dancing fun—but, again, ironically, and somewhat pathetically, because she became a blur: like countless others in the novel. The full-blown mock intrigue of the scene is apparent especially at the end when the New Yorker makes his exit while the narrator and the barmaid talk:

> The airplane man glared at her. Suddenly he jerked upright and roared (like the lion in the *Sports Afield* story?)—I thought first suit had stuck a knife in his back—then rushed her, arms extended as if to hug or strangle her. At the last instant, he swerved and hit the door, plunging into the night. (p. 61)

The obfuscation of the smoke in the barroom has become more ominously and mysteriously the night itself. By utilizing the vocabulary and incident of murder mystery and spy thriller, Welch, on the level of parody, is having great fun. But there is also the hint, created by the ambigous and ironic hopelessness the characters face, that the mystery and oblivion of night will, in keeping with the strain of naturalism in the novel, engulf them all.

◆

Thus the barmaid from Malta is lost in as much darkness of anonymity as is the New Yorker, and the narrator, and the two men in suits, and so is the old man, who in a later scene is identifed as a spy by the airplane man (one of a cadre of comic types in his pursuit), and who, after that identification, falls face first into his bowl of oatmeal. At this Welch's range of mock intrigue dramatizes the sad hilarity of life as a bad joke.

On several levels, then, the network of escapes and pursuits expands into a mass of comic tangles: the narrator pursues Agnes and at the same time flees from her brother and the redheaded cowboy whom the narrator helps Doagie roll; the New Yorker flees from his high-living past, pursued by the paranoia of real and imagined spies and FBI agents, and tries to make the narrator the instrument of his extravagant escape; grandmother, thinking of a paring knife, plots the assasination of Agnes as if she merits the stature of a long-standing Cree enemy. The "stacked" barmaid from Malta; Malvina, the woman in Harlem with the intriguing initials, "J.R." tattooed on her hand, and the mother of an inscrutable, sinister son about as comically threatening as the oatmeal man; Marlene, the rotten-toothed floozy who literally picks up the narrator from the sidewalks of Havre (echoing First Raise's position in the barrow pit)—all of these characters are introduced by Welch as laminations of the element of mock intrigue, but tend ultimately to merge always, and reciprocally, with the more tragic mysteries of the book.

Like all fine novels, *Winter in the Blood* invites new insights, new connections each time it is read. There are countless scenes, numerous elements that hold up again and again, analysis after analysis (both of and in spite of analysis). Read as a tragi-comedy about the confusions of life amplified through literature, it is possible to classify a main structural and thematic element in the novel as the interplay of mystery and mock intrigue.

And behind the humor and the pathos at each juncture in the Montana and mind journey of an anonymous American Indian narrator, is the author, James Welch, who although he knows the answers to the tragic mysteries and comic intrigues of his own novelistic creation, succeeds in communicating to the reader a modernist, at once realistic and surrealistic version of what Keats mysteriously termed, when looking not at Montana but at the Elgin Marbles, a "shadow of a magnitude."

Notes

---

[1]James Welch, *Winter in the Blood* (New York: Bantam, 1974). All future references to the novel are from this edition and are cited parenthetically. Other critics who have pointed to the comic aspects of the novel include: Charles R. Larson, *American Indian Fiction* (Albuquerque: University of New Mexico, 1978); Alan R. Velie, *Four American Indian Literary Masters* (Norman: University of Oklahoma, 1982); Peter Wild, *James Welch* (Boise; Western Writers Series, 1983); William F. Smith, "*Winter in the Blood:* The Indian Cowboy as Everyman," *Michigan Academician*, 10 (Winter 1978).

[2]In trying to understand how tragedy and comedy mingle in *Winter in the Blood*, Northrop Frye's scheme of four "Pregeneric plots," his four "Mythos or generic plots" provide one context. In Frye's system, *Winter in the Blood* might be regarded most generally as representative of "the mythos of winter: irony and satire." Frye says, "Tragedy and comedy

contrast rather than blend, and so do romance and irony, the champions respectively of the ideal and the actual. On the other hand, comedy blends insensibly into satire at one extreme and into romance at the other; romance may be comic or tragic; tragic extends from high romance to bitter and ironic realism." See Northrop Frye, *Anatomy of Criticism* (Princeton: Princeton Univ. Press, 1957), p. 162. Defining his "mythos of winter," Frye says, "the central principle of ironic myth is best approached as a parody of romance: the application of romantic mythical forms to a more realistic content which fits them in unexpected ways" (p. 223). And so it is with *Winter in the Blood.*

Alienation and the Female Principle in *Winter in the Blood*

◆

A. LaVonne Ruoff

> But the distance I felt came not from country or
> people; it came from within me. I was as distant from
> myself as the hawk from the moon. And that was why I
> had no particular feelings toward my mother and
> grandmother. Or the girl who had come to live with
> me (2).

In the words quoted above, the nameless[1] narrator of *Winter in the Blood* summarizes the sense of alienation which plagues him and which must be exorcized before he can become whole within himself and can close the distance he feels between himself and the external world. To do so, he undertakes a spiritual and physical journey into experience and memory to find the truth about his own feelings and about his family and girlfriend. Through most of the novel, the only people he really loves are his brother Mose and his father First Raise.[2] After Mose was killed by an automobile on the highway while the two boys were herding cattle back to the ranch, the narrator became a "servant to a memory of death"(38). Though the loss of the brother was immediate, the loss of his father was gradual. Following the accident, First Raise was home less and less often until he finally froze to death on a drunken binge. In the ten years since his father's death, the narrator has been able to do nothing of consquence. The closeness he feels to them contrasts with the distance he feels from the females in the novel—human and animal. This article will examine the causes and resolution of the narrator's sense of alienation through an analysis of the cultural context—traditional as well as contemporary—of his relationships with and characterizations of these females.

The chain of circumstances which ultimately leads to the narrator's feelings of separateness begins with his grandmother, who is at once the unwitting cause of the family's isolation from the Blackfeet tribe and the means by which the narrator can partially learn about them and his family. Despite the many stories about her early life which the grandmother told her young grandson, she revealed only part of the truth about her life with Standing Bear's band of Blackfeet. After his grandmother's death, the narrator obtains other parts of this story from blind, old Yellow Calf in order to determine the truth about her life and the identity of his own grandfather.

A beautiful girl thirty years younger than her husband, she slept with Chief Standing Bear only to keep him warm and to sing softly in his ear. The "bad medicine," which isolated not only the grandmother but also her descendants, began with the migration of her husband's band of Blackfeet from their traditional hunting grounds. After moving into Gros Ventre territory, they endured one of the hardest winters in memory. The details of the starvation winter of 1883-84 came from Yellow Calf, who lost all of his family to starvation and pneumonia.[3] After Standing Bear's death in a raid on the Gros Ventres, the young widow of not yet twenty was made an outcast by the band.[4] The grandmother attributed the women's action to their envy of her dark beauty. That of the men she attributed to their fear of the women's anger if they helped her and to their own reticence because of her position as Standing Bear's widow. However, Yellow Calf blames the mistreatment on a combination of physical, psychological, and religious causes:

> "She had not been with us more than a month or two, maybe, three. You must understand the thinking. In that time the soldiers came, the people had to leave their home up near the mountains, then the starvation and death of their leaders. She had brought them bad medicine"(154).

Her beauty, which had been a source of pride, now mocked them and their situation.

Thus, in the case of the grandmother, the source of alienation was external, resulting from circumstances beyond her control. Her isolation from the band became permanent when they were driven like cows by the soldiers to the new Blackfeet Reservation, established in 1888, the same year as the Fort Belknap Reservation was established for the Gros Ventres and Assiniboins. Because the band did not mention her to the soldiers and because she had moved a distance from the band in spring, the soldiers thought she was Gros Ventre.

In addition to attempting to determine the facts about the band's treatment of his grandmother, the narrator also tries to find out who hunted for her. Frustrated by Yellow Calf's refusal to answer his questions, the narrator suddenly realizes—at the moment his horse Bird farts—that Yellow Calf was that hunter. Solving this puzzle also solves those of the identity of his grandfather and of his own tribal heritage. At the beginning of the novel, the narrator explains that his grandmother "remained a widow for twenty-five years before she met a half-white drifter named Doagie, who had probably built this house where now the old lady snored and I lay awake thinking that I couldn't remember his face"(37). However, he does remember the rumors that Doagie was not his real grandfather.

Between the time she was abandoned by the Blackfeet band and the time she took in Doagie, the grandmother continued to live in isolation, separated by three miles from Yellow Calf, her secret visitor. Despite his realization of his grandfather's identity, the narrator cannot explain the distance between Yellow Calf and his grandmother: why the two waited twenty-five years after Standing Bear's death to procreate a child or why they continued to live separately afterward. Certainly the respect both had for Standing Bear is a very important part of the explanation. However, the theme of separation of males and females is repeated in the relationship between Teresa and First Raise and between the narrator and Agnes.[5] Another part of the explanation may be found in the traditional Blackfeet and Gros Ventre taboos against intermarriage within the band. Because the male members of the band were considered relatives, there was an old law against such intermarriage. By the time the bands were settled on the reservation, intermarriage was no longer considered a crime but was still bad form.[6] Consequently, when the grandmother (then about forty-five) and Yellow Calf conceived a child almost at the last opportunity before the onset of her menopause, they were violating a taboo in order to recreate a new generation of

Blackfeet in an alien land. Having done this, however, they chose to remain apart and the grandmother obscured the fatherhood of the child through living with Doagie. Nevertheless, this violation of custom was one more portion of the bad medicine passed on to the daughter Teresa.

The unwitting cause of the family's isolation from other Blackfeet, the grandmother still serves as its link to the tribe's culture and history. The power of the oral tradition she transmits is retained in the memory of the narrator. Advancing age has not diminished the strength of her contempt for those who made her an outcast or her hatred for such old enemies as the Crees. Too weak and feeble now even to chew regular food or to go to the toilet by herself, she is still fierce enough to wear a paring knife in her legging and plot ways to slit the throat of Agnes, her grandson's Cree girlfriend. Almost a hundred years old when the novel opens, the grandmother now communicates with her family with an occasional "ai" or squeak of her rocker.

In her silent old age, she must endure the vulgar teasing of Lame Bull,[7] in violation of the old Blackfeet and Gros Ventre taboo that a man should not speak to his mother-in-law or even look at her, a taboo equally binding on her. Also violated is the prohibition that although a mother-in-law might be supported by her son-in-law, she must not live in the same tepee with him but rather in a smaller one set at some distance away.[8] In addition the grandmother must endure the disinterest of her grandson, who usually regards her as a subject for bad jokes or detached curiosity. His treatment of her is a deviation from the traditional respect Indian children were expected to show elders.[9]

Though she clung to the old ways in life, the grandmother is denied them in death by her daughter, who insists that she be properly prepared for burial by the undertaker in near-by Harlem. Ironically, she is sealed up in her shiny coffin so that no one gets to see the undertaker's handiwork. Her funeral is neither Catholic nor traditional Blackfeet. Only her grandson observes a bit of the old burial customs by throwing onto her grave her one surviving possession from the old life—the tobacco pouch with its arrowhead. Having reached the end of his odyssey to find the truth about himself and his background, the narrator casts away the bundle representing the past.[10]

Teresa combines her mother's solemn dignity and fierce determination to survive with her own alienation from Blackfeet and Gros Ventre traditions. Because she rejected these in favor of acculturation, she is alienated both from the beliefs of her mother and the dreams and desires of her first husband and sons. The most valuable material possessions passed on to Teresa by her mother are the land acquired through mistaken identity and a house built by a man she wrongly believed to be her father. Although the ranch supports the family, it has destroyed what had been traditional Blackfeet and Gros Ventre role structure by making the male financially dependent on the female and by forcing the male to give up hunting for ranching to provide for his family. For solace and understanding, Teresa turns to Catholicism and to friendship with the Harlem priest, who makes Indians come to "his church, his saints and holy water, his feuding eyes" (5).

The differences between Teresa and the men in her family are revealed in her son's description of her as having always had "a clear bitter look, not without humor, that made others of us seem excessive, too eager to talk too much, drink too much, breathe too fast"(134-35). She approves hard work on the ranch and disapproves foolishness and fighting. Whatever natural intolerance she possesses has been sharpened by her experience with First Raise and her surviving son. As a result, she has developed the ability to interpret things as she wishes to see them and to ignore what she does not, as her memories of First Raise demonstrate. At the same time that she tells her son his father was not around enough, she insists that he accomplished what he set out to do. When her son points out her inconsistency, she merely says that he has mixed his father up with himself. Her only explanation of why First Raise stayed away so much is that he was a "foolish man" who "could never settle down"—a wanderer just like her son and "just like all these damned Indians" (19, 20).

Because Teresa is primarily concerned with doing what has to be done in order to provide for her family and to keep the ranch going, she marries Lame Bull shortly after her son arrives home from his latest spree in town. Clearly, she has no illusions about Lame Bull, whose advances she has previously resisted. When he jokes that her son has said she is ready to marry him, she replies in her clear, bitter voice that "my son tells lies that would make a weasel think twice. He was cut from the same mold as you" (9). Although after their marriage she complains about Lame Bull's sloppy habits and his teasing of her mother, she is obviously sexually attracted to him. Lame Bull only responds to her complaints by grinning a silent challenge, and "the summer nights came alive in the bedroom off the kitchen. Teresa must have liked his music" (23).

Her relationship with her son is complicated both by her own personality and by his inner turmoil. Like his father, whom he describes as "always in transit" (21) before his death, the narrator can neither live with Teresa nor leave her permanently. The conflict between mother and son is clear from Teresa's first words after he arrives home. Immediately accosting him with the news that his "wife" accidently took off with his gun and electric razor shortly after he lelft for town, she simultaneously urges him to get his property back and defends herself for not stopping the girl: "What did you expect me to do? I have your grandmother to look after, I have no strength, and she is young—Cree!" (3).

Her tactic of squeezing into one breath as much advice, criticism, and self defense as possible only antagonizes and further alienates her son.[11] Because she feels that her son's only real problems are that he is a wanderer like all Indians and that he is too sensitive, she cannot understand why he didn't stay on at the Tacoma hospital, where he was offered a job after having an operation on his leg. His explanation that he was hired only as a token Indian male to help the hospital qualify for grant money does not penetrate her consciousness. His bitterness at her lack of understanding is summed up in his comment that "I never expected much of Teresa and I never got it. But neither did anybody else. Maybe that's why First Raise stayed away so much" (21).

The narrator's discussion with Teresa about his pet duck, Amos, which precedes their discussion of First Raise and of the narrator himself, dramatically reveals the nature and possible consequences of their conflict. It is Teresa who reminds her son about Amos, and her habitually negative recollections become a springboard for her running commentary about her first husband, sons, and Indians in general. She recalls that First Raise won Amos by pitching pennies at the fair when "he was so drunk that he couldn't even see the plates" and that the other ducklings drowned because her sons did not keep the tub full of water for them—"You boys were like that " (15). When the narrator tries to explain that Amos, who had remained perched on the edge of the tub while his siblings plunged to the bottom, survived because he was smarter than the other ducklings, she dismisses his theory with the remark that "He was lucky. One duck can't be smarter than another. They're like Indians" (15). As far as she was concerned, the other ducks were crazy.

Like the narrator, Amos inexplicably survived a disastrous accident which killed his siblings. The narrator is just as unable to solve this puzzle as he is that of his own survival when his brother, Mose, died. Nevertheless, he does, in the course of this conversation with Teresa, learn that she killed Amos—a truth so horrifying that he desperately tries to avoid comprehending it. When he realizes that the answer to the question of who killed Amos, one he did not want to ask, is going to be either his mother or First Raise, he is so traumatized by the implications that he tries to suggest, instead, that one or the other of them killed the hated turkey which used to attack him. Teresa matter-of-factly leads her son to a truth he does not want to face but must if he is to make his peace with the past, accept the necessity of the sacrifice, and become a mature adult who now ceases to be dependent on her: the truth that she killed his pet, whom he and the family ate for Christmas dinner. In her own eyes, she has done what her husband and sons could not do—sacrifice sentiment for practicality by killing the pet duck for dinner.

Her act symbolizes the reversal of the traditional Indian male and female roles: because the hunter now can only dream of bringing elk meat home from Glacier Park, the mother is forced to provide food by whatever means available. However, her act has larger religious significance as well. As William Thacheray points out in "Crying for Pity in *Winter in the Blood,*" Teresa's killing of the duck is a ritual in which she forces her son to sacrfice what he holds most dear. He becomes a participant in the sacrifice when he unknowingly eats his pet. Such a sacrifice is part of the "Crying for Pity" ceremony which Thackeray demonstrates informs the structure of *Winter in the Blood.* The killing of the duck would have been especially abhorent to First Raise. The duck was sacred to the Gros Ventres because of its association with the primeval making of dry land.[12] Ironically, Teresa sacrifices a Gros Ventre religious symbol to celebrate the birth of Christianity's most sacred symbol.

Facing the fact that Teresa killed the duck helps the narrator recognize that his mother holds the power of life and death over him just as she held it over the duck. His unconsious recognition of this fact is revealed symbolically as he recalls his dream after the sexual encounter with the barmaid from Malta. In this dream, Teresa gives birth to the duck.

The conflict between mother and son is intensified by the intrusion of the opposite sex. Although Teresa treats Agnes with cold politeness because she thinks the girl is her son's wife, she does not hesitate to point out that the girl is not happy and belongs in town, which the narrator realizes means Agnes belongs in bars. Consequently, Teresa disapproves of her son's wanting to bring Agnes back. Teresa's marriage to Lame Bull and her friendship with the Harlem priest increase the narrator's hostility toward his mother. He cannot bear to see his father replaced by Lame Bull, whom he detests as a crafty, vulgar clown and whom he thinks married his mother for her ranch. Realizing that marriage to Lame Bull means that her son must leave, Teresa tells her son to start looking around because there is not enough for him on the ranch. Once again, Teresa attempts to wean her son and force him to go out on his own.

The narrator also cannot bear his mother's drinking partnership with the priest. When the latter sends Teresa a letter, the narrator wants to read it "to see what a priest would have to say to a woman who was his friend. I had heard of priests having drinking partners, fishing partners, but never a woman partner" (58). Instead, because he cannot even bring himself to see her name inside the envelope, he tears the letter up between his legs—an act with Oedipal overtones.

The Oedipal jealousy he feels is part of his inability to separate himself from her and to see himself and his mother as they really are rather than as his distorted perception makes them seem. The narrator's view is not held by everybody. When the bartender in Malta comments that Teresa is "a good one—one of the liveliest little gals I know of," the narrator wryly comments that "She is bigger than you are, bigger than both of us together" (56). The best example of the tender side of her nature is her care and love for her mother. The narrator is so self-absorbed and distanced from his mother that he has no perception of how hard the physical and psychological drain of running the ranch, raising her family, and caring for an aged mother have been on Teresa.

Now fifty-six years old, Teresa is worn down by the endless demands on her by a mother almost a hundred years old and a son of thirty-two whose chief occupation seems to be getting drunk, laid, and beaten up. Her acts of genuine caring and her grief over the death of her mother contrast with the behavior of both the narrator and Lame Bull. Rather than join her new husband and her son in drinking *Vin Rose'* after the grandmother's grave is dug, she walks into her bedroom to be alone. During the bizarre funeral, she falls to her knees in grief. The narrator's slowly increasing perception of the hard lives of both his grandmother and mother is reflected in his growing awareness that Teresa has come to resemble her mother. How much she differs from his one-night stands is revealed in his comment, made while digging the grandmother's grave, that "from this distance she looked big and handsome, clean-featured, unlike the woman I had seen the night before" (137).

Deprived of the affection he needs from Teresa, the narrator seeks it in a misplaced attachment to Agnes and casual sexual encounters. Because Agnes is a Cree from Havre, scorned by the reservation people, a permanent union with her would continue the bad medicine passed down from the narrator's grandmother. The narrator vividly recalls the stories she has told him about the Crees, who were good only for the whites who had slaughtered Indians, had served as scouts for the soldiers, and "had learned to live like them, drink with them and the girls who had opened their thighs to the Long Knives. The children of these unions were doubly cursed in the eyes of the old woman"(33).

The contempt of the Blackfeet for the Crees was based not only on their long-standing warfare and on the Crees' close interaction with the whites but also on their strikingly opposed attitudes toward female sexual morality. Among the Crees, chastity was desirable but not essential, and illegitimacy was not a cause of great concern. An adulterous wife might be given to the lover in exchange for a gift, and wife exchange operated similarly (Mandelbaum 37.2:245-47).

Among the Blackfeet, chastity was of supreme importance. Because illegitimate pregnancy was regarded as a severe family disgrace, young girls were closely watched by their mothers and married off as soon as possible after puberty. Women's prayers uniformly began with the declaration of their purity; and the most important ceremonial, the Sun Dance, began with the vow of a virtuous woman for the recovery of the sick. On the other hand, the Blackfeet male's efforts at seduction were actively encouraged by his family.[13] Perhaps because of this double standard, the Blackfeet

traded with the Crees for love medicine, which the former called
Ito-wa-mami-wa-natsi or Cree medicine (McClintock 190). Chastity
was similarly prized by the Gros Ventres. The institution of the child
bride, given in marriage before puberty, and polygyny characterized
Gros Ventre marriages up to about 1880. The Gros Ventres believed
that a girl could not menstruate until after she had experienced sexual
intercourse. Consequently, if a girl had her first menses before
marriage, her family was disgraced (Flannery, *The Gros Ventres of
Montana* 15.1:171).

Agnes' conduct, as well as her tribal background, reinforces the
conclusion that the narrator has made a disastrous choice. Agnes is
interested only in exchanging sex for a good time and whatever she
can get or steal. As the narrator puts it, she is "a fish for dinner,
nothing more" (22). When she grew bored reading movie magazines
and imagining she looked like Raquel Welch, she took the narrator's
gun and electric razor and headed for Malta, where she quickly found
a new man. Despite his recognition that she is "Cree and not worth a
damn" (33), the narrator is haunted by the image of her body by
moonlight, a memory stronger than the experience itself. Because he
cannot get her out of his blood, he hesitatingly decides to go after her.

Like the medicine man Fish, whose interpretation of the signs
after Standing Bear's death was partially responsible for making the
grandmother an outcast from her band, Agnes possesses a power
which cannot be withstood: her "fish medicine" is strong enough to
separate the narrator from his grandmother and mother. He longs to
recapture what he has convinced himself that he and Agnes had
together before she left. But when the narrator finally finds her in
Havre, he hides so that she cannot see him: "I wanted to be with her,
but I didn't move. I didn't know how to go to her. There were people
counting on me to make her suffer, and I too felt that she should suffer
a little. Afterwards, I could buy her a drink" (102).

This same ambivalence is demonstrated in his physical descriptions of her. He is attracted by her combination of open sexuality and
childlike innocence. When he meets her in a bar, she is wearing a dress
cut almost to the waist in back and pulled up over her thighs.
Nevertheless, her eyes "held the promise of warm things, of a spirit
that went beyond her miserable life of drinking and screwing and men
like me" (113). Because of his growing desire to reform himself and to
believe that she really is capable of warmth and affection, he tries to

persuade her to settle down by learning a trade like shorthand. Although she curtly rejects his advice in disbelief, his attempt to reform her is an essential step toward achieving his own regeneration because he had expressed concern for the welfare of someone with whom he wants a close relationship: "I was calm, but I didn't feel good. Maybe it was a kind of love" (132). Unfortunately, Agnes's reaction to his plaintive confession that he is not happy leaves no doubt that he will get even less sympathy from her than he has from Teresa: "That's a good one. Who is?" (113).

Neither her rejection of his suggestion for a new life nor the beating administered by her brother breaks the bond which ties him to her. Although he lies to his inquisitive neighbor, Mrs. Frederick Horn, when he tells her that Agnes came back with him, he obviously intends to try to fulfill his wish. By the end of the novel, he has healed enough internally to think about going to a doctor about his injured knee but not enough to risk losing Agnes by taking the time necessary to recover from surgery. His need to end the spiritual and emotional pain of his longing for her is stronger than his need to end the physical pain in his knee: "Next time I'd do it right. Buy her a couple of cremes de menthe, maybe offer to marry her on the spot" (175). Given the evidence about Agnes's attitudes and behavior, his wish for stability and closeness through marriage is not likely to be fulfulled. He may catch his "fish" again, but he probably will not be able to hang onto her. However, his wanting a close relationship with a woman, even if he has to commit himself to marriage, demonstrates how far he has progressed from the distance he felt within himself and from the women in his life which he expressed at the beginning of the novel.

While tracking down his missing girlfriend, the narrator meets Malvina, who represents what Agnes will probably be like at forty. However, Malvina, unlike Agnes, has tried to make something of herself by taking a two-year secretarial course at Haskell Institute, a government Indian school. Unfortunately, she never found a job as a secretary. When the narrator meets her in a Harlem bar, she is tough and aggressive in her disgust at the older men's conversation, her demand that they buy her a drink and her successful attempt to pick up the narrator. She offers him neither affection nor unlimited sex. Her cocoon-like bedrom is carefully furnished to give the illusion of sensuality. The many pictures of her smiling in earlier days contrast with her present toughness. The globes of bubble-bath remind the narrator of the unused ones in Teresa's bedroom given her by First Raise. Although the sensuality of Malvina's bedroom and voluptuousness of her body arouse renewed desire in the narrator, she verbally castrates him for wanting more than she is willing to give. Her sharp commands to "beat it" (84) freeze first his hand reaching between her thighs and then his groin. Like Teresa and Agnes, Malvina has cut him off.

The characterization of the female as castrator is graphically dramatized by Belva Long Knife, who owns her ranch and is perhaps the best cowboy in her family, including her son Raymond, who won a silver belt buckle for "All-around Cowboy, Wolf Point Stampede, 1954" (26). After wrestling calves to the ground and castrating them, she would throw the testicles into the fire: "She made a point of eating the roasted balls while glaring at one man, then another—even her sons, who, like the rest of us, stared at the brown hills until she was done" (24). The economic power of women over men is seen as a less dramatic form of castration. Emily Short, for example, has the best fields on the reservation because she serves on the tribal council. The combined image of sexual and economic power of the women is demonstrated in the complaint of the gas station attendant to the narrator that he cannot fire his helper who is more intent on masturbation than work because "his old lady'd cut my nuts off" (75). The power of wives over their husbands is shown both in the example of the regular bartender in Malta who is not working because he has wife troubles and in that of the airplane man who was reported to the FBI by his wife for embezzlement.

The anonymous barmaid from Malta represents another experience in sexual frustration. Her namelessness emphasizes how insignificant she is to the men in the bar attracted by her hips and breasts. To them she is a "nice little twitch" (50), an object to devour with their eyes and to compare with their wives. Even the nameless and mysterious embezzler, the airplane man, for whom she used to dance, cannot place or identify her. For the narrator, she becomes more than an object of lust because she involves him in additional searches for truth to determine her past relationship with the airplane man and to find out what happened between her and the narrator in the hotel.

As he gradually awakens with a hangover the morning after meeting the barmaid, he recalls his dream filled with images of sexual abuse of the barmaid and his mother. In this dream, which serves as a kind of vision, the elements of his past experience form a montage of destruction and regeneration foreshadowing experiences to come. He first describes the image of a girl slit and gutted like a rainbow trout, begging men to turn her loose. She then becomes the bar maid, screaming under the hands of leering men. In the last image, she is a gutted fish fallen upon by men. Despite the specific allusion to the barmaid, the implied allusion to Agnes, his particular "fish," is clear.

The images of Teresa present her as a sexual victim and a person with both verbal and procreative power. She is described as hanging upside down from a wanted man's belt, which becomes the narrator's, in a helpless sexual position with strong Oedipal overtones. Next she is described as being fondled by the men who comment on her body as they spread her legs wider and wider until Amos waddles out and soars up into the dull sun, which is the most sacred deity (Na'to's) of the Blackfeet. Among the Gros Ventres, the sun is not identified with the Supreme Being but is regarded as his property, work, and servant. The sun does not have the religious predominance it has among the Blackfeet. In terms of both Blackfeet and Gros Ventres traditions, Amos, the animal which has appeared to the narrator in his dream, has become his medicine or secret helper.[14]

The instrument of Amos's death has become the means of his rebirth in the dream. Symbolically, the instrument of the narrator's physical birth and spiritual death has become the means of his rebirth. By releasing her son, Teresa frees him to soar out of her grasp. The act foreshadows the rebirth of the narrator later in the novel. However, Teresa is not described as being so helpless as the barmaid. In addition to having the power to give birth, she also has the vocal power to warn the airplane man and to rage at the narrator. Further, her voice, which the narrator does not escape in the dream, becomes the medium to carry him from this episode to the next, which involves the boys' driving the cattle back to the ranch. The emphasis on the power of her voice indicates both his acceptance of her verbal domination and his need for her assistance in recalling images from his own memory. It also contrasts with his inability to communicate in the dream because his guts are spilling out of his monstrous mouth. The image foreshadows his verbally spilling out his anguish when trying to pull the cow out of the slough.

After awakening from the dream, the narrator cannot remember whether or not he had intercourse with the Malta barmaid. However, he gradually remembers being in bed with her and seeing her body, especially the image of the button strained between her breasts. Despite his inability to remember the details of the episode, its significance in terms of the development of his ability to care about someone else is shown in his feeling almost ashamed that he might have intruded on her relationship with the airplane man.

His recollection of her coming to his room at the hotel returns when the sight of her hips from the rear rouses his sexual desire and the memory of popping the button between her breasts. His reactions to the barmaid in terms of parts of her anatomy indicate the fragmented state of his mind, which makes him as incapable of effectively reestablishing contact with the barmaid as he was with Agnes. Because he does not know her name and realizes the clerk of the hotel she has entered will not help him he is overcome with helpless frustration in a "world of stalking white men" and violent Indians: "I was a stranger to both and both had beaten men" (200). After waiting two hours for the barmaid to come down from her room, he gives up in despair and picks up Marlene, who becomes the victim of his frustrated lust.

Ironically, Marlene is the woman who shows him the most sympathy. The contrast between her compassion and Agnes's indifference toward the narrator is heightened by the fact that Marlene is probably Cree like Agnes. Thackeray notes that "Marlene" is a familiar given name among the Cree-Metis of the area (45). Bulky with teeth blacked around the edges, Marlene makes up in compassion what she lacks in beauty. When she first sees him on the sidewalk after he has been beaten, she both expresses concern and offers to get him something to drink. Later, when he has taken her to a dingy hotel, her eyes water every time she looks at his swollen eyes. Although she allows him to hide in the softness of her body, he feels no similar compassion for her. In his state of frustration and alienation, he perceives her merely as his "great brown hump" (121) and as an object to be examined like a scientific specimen.

When he covers her with his own body, she becomes to him the symbol of the three women who have frustrated him sexually—Agnes, Malvina, and the barmaid. Her repeated requests for him to "kiss my pussy" (121,123) cause him to explode into violence, slapping her hard and then holding her down so that she cannot move. He feels no emotion as he watches her sob. Nevertheless, the act of violence has brought him a kind of peace because he does not feel the need for anything, even sex. No longer the receiver of violence at the hands of the white rancher at the beginning of the novel or of Agnes's brother, he has transmitted the violence from within his spirit onto the body of someone weaker than he. Unable to communicate his anger and frustration verbally, he resorts to communicating through blows. This act of violence frees him from being so driven by frustrated lust that he cannot cope with the other problems in his life. Although she struggles against him, Marlene harbors no strong resentment. Because his treatment of her seems only to remind her of how sick he is and because her loneliness causes her to seek companionship, whatever the cost, she offers to forego any money he might give her to persuade him to stay and talk with her.

The effect of the release of his pent-up frustration is shown in the sympathy he feels for the small, sickly daughter of the Michigan professor with whom he gets a ride home after leaving Marlene. Noticing that the child is frail and white, with eyes as dull as a calf's, he gradually becomes aware that she suffers some kind of discomfort, which causes her parents to stop the car so that she can vomit. After the girl comes out from behind the bushes, he returns her smile, forgetful of the pain the act of smiling will cause his swollen nose. He performs a final act of graciousness when he allows her father to take his picture before leaving the family.

His compassion for her continues after their separation, as exemplified by his eating, more out of loyalty than hunger, the peach she gave him. His odyssey now over, he has come full circle back to his home, and having been able to feel some measure of sympathy for someone other than himself, he is ready to take the final steps to close the distance within himself. That these final steps will necessitate death and the threat of death in order to bring back the full memory of the accident which killed Mose and the exorcism of the bad medicine in his family's blood is evident from his recollection on his way home of killng the hawk as a boy out hunting with Mose. The allusion to the hawk, to which he compared himself at the beginning of the novel, emphasizes the circular nature of his odyssey. The description of the dying hawk's futile efforts to communicate, parallel those of the narrator.

Although the women and the young girl figure in the causes and resolution of the narrator's alienation, they are not the only females whose actions affect him. Two crucial incidents in the novel involve cows. The death of Mose in a car accident, a major cause of his alienation, resulted from the actions of a wild-eyed spinster cow. Sent by First Raise to round up the cattle for the winter, the twelve-year-old narrator and his fourteen-year-old brother rush to herd back all the cattle in one day. The physical appearance of the wild-eyed cow and her spinsterhood in a herd consisting primarily of mothers with calves set her apart from the others, just as the grandmother in her youth was set apart from her band because of her appearance and childlessness. Avoiding the calves with outraged dignity, the wild-eyed cow ran across the valley and raced headlong down the incline across the highway. Inexplicably, she refused to go through the gate on the other side, which caused the cattle behind her to bunch up along the highway. When a speeding car killed Mose, the narrator did not even see the accident because his horse Bird had bolted after a stray calf. The narrator was thrown to the ground, injuring his knee, after Bird jolted down the shoulder of the highway.

Despite the fact that the narrator always associates the wild-eyed cow with the accident, he realizes that, as an instrument of an uncontrollable fate, she is no more to blame than the boys themselves. His acceptance of this signals his growing awareness that perhaps Teresa was no more to blame for the destruction of the family unit and his own sense of disorientation than is himself. Nevertheless, the accident was ultimately responsible for the loss of the only two people he really loved—his brother and father.

Twenty years after the accident, this wild-eyed cow becomes the means of the narrator's regeneration.[15] The mother cow and her calf serve as a focus for his readaptation to ranch life after the violence of the town. The chores he performs for them provide an opportunity to feel concern and commitment for something other than himself and thus provide a transitional stage to the development of these feelings for humans. Further, the mother cow's stubborn refusal to be separated from her calf and its dependence on her can be compared with the relationship the narrator has with his mother and that many of the children in the novel have with theirs. Although Teresa, unlike the cow, recognizes that she must wean her son, she still continues to be concerned about him. In contrast, Malvina seems to show little concern for the destructive impact her lovers will have on her son.

Similar parental indifference is evident toward the two small children left alone in the car. Parental abandonment through death is described in the magazine story about the pregnant woman killed in Africa whose child is born alive, a story the narrator reads at the beginning of the novel. Animals, such as the mare and her colt which the narrator sees as the novel opens, seem to care more for their young than do humans.

The attempts of the mother cow and her calf to get together recur throughout the novel and their cries to one another provide transitions into various episodes. When the narrator is attempting to convince Lame Bull that he was an adult of twenty when the flood occurred, among the sounds he hears are the mother cow's answering from the slough the cries of her calf. Its cries throughout the novel echo those of the narrator, who whines in anguish over his own separation from loved ones and over his unwillingness to move past the dependence of childhood and adolescence to the independence of adulthood.

One of his first chores in the novel is to shoo the sucking calf away from its mother. When the calf erupts under the narrator's arm as he pins it against the fence, the touch of its thigh triggers his first memory of childhood—that of riding calves with his brother. Although he chases the cow back to the slough, he knows she will be back because her udder is full. Later, the tender sight of the cow's licking the head of her calf in the corral precedes his conversation with Teresa about Amos, First Raise, and himself. The sudden bawling of the calf interrupts his memory of how the ducks drowned. When the narrator tries to saddle old Bird and ride out to visit Yellow Calf for the first time, the calf follows the bucking horse and rider out of the corral, not sure whether to go with them or return to its mother. Its confusion parallels that of the narrator.

The sound of the calf's bawling at feeding time catches the narrator's attention before he sees the mother up to her chest in mud. The narrator's attempts to get her out become his epic battle for the possession of truth and of his own soul, for which he has been purified by a ritual bath shortly before the episode and by his visit to the trickster-holy man, Yellow Calf. Temporarily overcome with hatred for what the wild-eyed, equally stupid and hateful cow did to his life, he nonetheless realizes that he must risk re-injuring his knee and possible death by wading out into the mud to save this cow. Out of his intense physical effort, prolonged by Bird's initial disinclination to help, come the ability to verbalize his anger and self pity and the ability to perceive that his mother—like everybody—has been taken for a ride:

> Your husband, your friends, your son, all worthless,
> none of them worth a shit. Slack up, you sonofabitch!
> Your mother dead, your father—you don't even know,
> what do you think of that? A joke, can't you see? Lame
> Bull! The biggest joke—can't you see that he's a joke, a
> joker playing a joke on you? Were you taken for a ride!
> Slack up, slack up! This greedy stupid country--(169).

Renewed through his verbalization and revelation, he finds the strength first to plan a new life and then to try to finish the job of hauling the cow out of the mud with the help of old Bird, who dies in the attempt. The narrator's sacrifice for the cow, though apparently unsuccessful, makes him feel closer to Mose and First Raise, although he has rejected the temptation of joining them in death by allowing himself to sink into the grave in the mud. He also feels closer to nature, enjoying the sensation of the cleansing, summer rain. Both cow and calf are silent, the mother presumably dead and the calf weaned. The narrator is now ready to make his final peace with his grandmother's bad medicine, his mother, and himself and to propose one with Agnes. The winter in his blood has thawed.

Notes

[1] An earlier version of this article appeared in *The American Indian Quarterly*, 4(1978), pp. 107-22. Although I have revised portions of the article and the notes, the substance remains essentially the same. The information on the Blackfeet, Gros Ventres, and Crees in the notes has been taken from my "History in *Winter in the Blood*: Backgrounds and Bibliography," which appeared in the same issue (pp. 169-72). All page references are to the hardback edition of the novel (New York: Harper, 1974).

In addition to using the device of the anonymous narrator to indicate alienation and universality, as have many other novelists, Welch may also use it to allude to the traditional reluctance of members of the Blackfeet, Gros Ventres, and Plains tribes to tell their names for fear it will bring bad luck. For descriptions of Blackfeet reluctance to give their names, see Walter McClintock, *The Old North Trail* (1910; rpt. Lincoln: University of Nebraska Press, 1968), p. 395, and George Bird Grinnell, *Blackfoot Lodge Tales* (1892; rpt. Lincoln: University of Nebraska Press, 1962), p. 194. In his *Ethnology of the Gros Ventre*, A. L. Kroeber notes that some of the Gros Ventres were ashamed to speak their own names (Anthropological Papers of the American Museum of Natural History, 1.4 (1908) p. 182;). In his autobiography *From the Deep Woods to Civilization*, Charles Alexander Eastman describes the futile efforts of his white teacher to get him to tell his name: "Evidently he had not been among the Indians long, or he would not have asked that question. It takes a tactician and a diplomat to get an Indian to tell his name!" (1916; rpt. Lincoln: University of Nebraska Press, 1977, 22).

When he gives readings from the novel, James Welch sometimes comments, perhaps with tongue in cheek, that the narrator has no name because the author forgot to give him one.

[2] First Raise is presumably Gros Ventre. William Thackeray notes that First Raise and Lame Bull (the narrator's stepfather) are common surnames at Fort Belknap. Mose and Teresa are familiar given names ("Crying for Pity in *Winter in the Blood,*" 45). Although the grandmother is Blackfeet by blood and culture, the narrator is undoubtedly considered Gros Ventre by the reservation people both because his father is a member of that tribe and because the narrator was raised among the Gros Ventres. For this reason, I have cited both Blackfeet and Gros Ventre world views and customs in explaining allusions in the novel.

According to Sidner J. Larson, who shares a common set of grandparents with Welch, First Raise is partially modeled on Welch's uncle James O'Bryan. A frequent visitor to nearby bars, James was killed in an automobile accident while returning home one night. See "James Welch's *Winter in the Blood,*" *The Indian Historian*, 10 (1977): p. 24.

[3] There is considerable confusion over the definition of the term "Blackfeet" and over their relationship to the Gros Ventres. These tribes were referred to as "The Blackfoot Nation" in the treaty signed in Judith Basin in 1855. The term "The Blackfoot Nation" is a misnomer because it refers to four tribes temporarily allied at that time: Northern Blackfeet (Siksika), Bloods (Kainah), Piegans, and Gros Ventres. Although the first three were operating as separate tribes by the time of white contact, they believed themselves to have a common descent; they also continued to speak the same dialect of Algonkian, to share similar customs, and to war against the same enemies. However, they did not consider the Gros Ventres to have an origin common with theirs.

The Gros Ventres, known also by the Blackfeet name "Atsina" and a

version of their Cree name, "Fall" or "Water-Fall" Indians, spoke an
Algonkian dialect so different from that of the Blackfeet that the groups
could understand one another only with difficulty. The Gros Ventres are
considered to have once been part of the Arapahos, another Algonkian
tribe. Although the Blackfeet, Arapahos, and Gros Ventres were among
the older Algonkian residents of the Plains, evidence points to the
Blackfeet as the earliest of these.

By the beginning of the eighteenth century, the Blackfeet dominated
the Northwestern Plains between the Missouri and Saskatchewan Rivers.
This area became the scene of constant intertribal warfare from the time
of white contact until 1887. The Gros Ventres, established in the late
seventeenth century between the forks of the Saskatchewan River, were
gradually driven south by the Crees and Assiniboins into closer proximity
with the Blackfeet. Known as the most warlike Indians of the Northern
Plains, the Blackfeet were feared by Indians and whites alike, particularly
when allied with the Gros Ventres. One of the goals of the 1855 treaty was
to protect surrounding tribes by delineating the hunting territory to be
common to the three tribes of Blackfeet and the Gros Ventres. New
warfare, however, resulted from rekindled hostility towards whites.
Between 1862 and 1877, the Northern Blackfeet, Bloods, and Northern
Piegans withdrew into Canada and were assigned reservations in
Alberta, leaving only the Southern Piegans in Montana. These Piegans
are the Blackfeet in *Winter in the Blood*.

The virtual extermination of the buffalo by the late 1870's made
game scarce both in Canada and in the United States. By the winter of
1882, the remaining buffalo in Montana were in the Gros Ventre territory
between the Milk River and the Bear Paw Mountains. Competition for the
disappearing game came not only from Montana Indians but also from
the Canadian Blackfeet, Crees, and Assiniboins, who came down after
game had disappeared in their own country. The end of the nomadic life
for the Southern Piegans, Gros Ventres, and Assiniboins came as a result
of the starvation winter of 1883-84, the pivotal event which both the
grandmother and Yellow Calf recall in *Winter in the Blood*. Their
recollections of the suffering of that period are corroborated by
contemporary accounts. During that winter, over four hundred of the
Southern Piegans—who remained buffalo hunters to the end—starved to
death. When Major Reuben Allen, appointed Blackfeet agent in April
1884, entered twenty-three lodges, the only food he found that day was one
small rabbit and a steer's hoof. Under the leadership of White Calf, their
head chief since 1877, the Southern Piegans offered to exchange gameless
land for necessities. Having endured equal hardships, the Gros Ventres
and Assiniboins reached similar conclusions. Subsequent investigations

and negotiations finally culminated in the establishment by the United States government in May 1888 of the Blackfeet Reservation for the Southern Piegans and the Fort Belknap Reservation for the Gros Ventres and Upper Assiniboins. See John Ewers, *The Blackfeet: Raiders of the Northwestern Plains* (Norman: University of Oklahoma Press, 1958), and *Ethnological Report on the Blackfeet and Gros Ventre Tribes of Indians,* American Indian Ethnohistory: Plains Indians (New York:Garland, 1974), pp. 3, 21, 93-94, 123-26, 130, 150-55.

[4] A Blackfeet myth explaining the origin of the Blackfeet describes men and women as living separately. Old Man (Na'pi), a creator-trickster figure in Blackfeet mythology, brought them together so that they could continue and so that the men would abandon their lazy dissolute ways and learn from the women's example of orderly self government and mastery of agriculture and domestic arts. In this tale, Old Man outsmarts himself and ends up without a mate. He wanted to take Chief woman for his wife. However, when she tested him by appearing disguised in dirty, ragged clothes, he rejected her. In revenge, she chose instead a handsome young bachelor. The endings to the story vary. In the version recorded by John Mason Brown, the Blackfeet sprang from the union of Chief Woman and the young man. Enraged at her trick and her selection of a husband, Old Man sentenced all women to serve men—a state of affairs obviously reversed in Welch's novel. See Brown, "Traditions of the Blackfeet," *Galaxy* 3(1867): pp. 157-61; copy in Newberry Library, Chicago.

[5] For discussions of the Blackfeet taboo on band intermarriage, see Clark Wissler, *The Social Life of the Blackfoot Indians,* Anthropological Papers of the American Museum of Natural History, 7.1(New York, 1900): pp. 19-20; Grinnell 211; McClintock 187. For discussions of the Gros Ventre taboo, see Kroeber, 1.4:147, and Regina Flannery, *The Gros Ventres of Montana,* The Catholic University of America Anthropological Series, 15.1(Washington, D.C., 1953): pp. 29-31.

[6] Larson states that "Lame Bull" is the name of the novelist's Gros Ventre grandfather, James Smith O'Bryan. Larson indicates that the grandfather used to ask his wife the same question the narrator asks his grandmother: "Old woman, do you want some music?" (p. 11). See Larson p. 24.

[7] For explanations of the Blackfeet customs toward mothers-in-law, see Wissler, 7.1:12-13; Grinnell 195; McClintock 187. For explanations of the Gros Ventre customs, see Kroeber, 1.4:180. Flannery notes that "the respect between members of the opposite sex who are of contiguous generations was most apparent in the avoidance between mother-in-law and son-in-law. This required that the two neighbors neither look at nor speak to each other any time" (15.1:109).

[8] For a description of Blackfeet child-raising customs, see Wissler, 7.1:29-30, and Grinnell 189. According to Flannery, the relationship between Gros Ventre grandparents and grandchildren was free and easy, "unmarked by the reticence which characterized the parent-child relationship, or by the feeling of restraint which obtains between so many relatives of opposite sex" (15.1: 121). Grandparents were indulgent toward their grandchildren and joking between the two groups was common. Because the Gros Ventre believed that an old person had been privileged to do so by the Supreme Being, they concluded that if you are good to the old, they will pray to the Supreme Being for your health, long life, and success. Children were instructed to be good to the aged as well as ask them for their prayers (15.1:122, 195).

[9] Geri Rhodes interprets this act as throwing away the bad medicine that has haunted the grandmother since she was cast out by her band ("*Winter in the Blood*—Bad Medicine in the Blood," *New American*, Special Native American Issue, 2 (1976), pp. 44-49. I do not agree with this interpretation. The narrator is following a burial custom common to both the Blackfeet and Gros Ventre—that of burying with the deceased the possession he or she most valued in life.

[10] Flannery comments that oral instruction or lecturing was the most important Gros Ventre method of child training. All of her middle-aged and older informants agreed that some relative, usually the mother or father, daily lectured their children about right and wrong. Lecturing started when the child was an infant and continued until adulthood was attained. Children were expected to listen and to retain a respectful attitude (15.1: 165-64).

[11] The earthdiver myth is one of the most common North American Indian myths. William Thackeray discusses the cultural and literary significance of the animals in his excellent "Animal Allies and Transformers in *Winter in the Blood*, *MELUS*, 12:2 (Summer 1985) forthcoming. The Flat Pipe, one of the Gros Ventre's most sacred ceremonial objects, has a bowl shaped like the head of a duck. The Flat pipe bundle contains not only the pipe itself but a turtle shell, "duck" pelt, and muskrat skin. These represent the animals sent by Earthmaker after the great flood to dive for earth. Only turtle and "duck" returned with earth. The "duck" is apparently a grebe, sacred both because of its role in making dry land and in present-day bird migration. See Cooper 16.2:pp. 60-72.

[12] The hatred of the grandmother and the antagonism of Teresa to Agnes, the narrator's Cree girlfriend, is rooted in the history of the Plains Crees. Originally a woodland tribe, the Crees had early contact with whites. After the establishment of trading posts in their territory in Canada, the Crees became dependent upon trade goods, especially liquor and guns, and served as middlemen to white traders. Using their guns to push back enemies like the Blackfeet and Gros Ventres, they moved westward onto the prairies between 1740 and 1820 to trap beaver. For the next sixty years, the Plains Crees waged unceasing war on the Blackfeet. Their commerce with the whites contrasted sharply with the ferocity with which the Blackfeet opposed them.

The group that eventually settled in Montana was the southern-most band of the Canadian Plains Crees, the Cree-Assiniboins, so named because of their close relationship and intermarriage with the Assiniboins. The American-born Rocky Boy (or Stone Child) and his band of Chippewas attached themselves to this group. Fragmented bands of mixed-bloods, Crees, and Chippewas (primarily refugees from Louis Riel's unsuccessful rebellion of 1885) wandered hungry and homeless all over Montana in the 1890's. For a brief period, some were placed on the Blackfeet Reservation, where they were made to feel unwelcome. The Canadian Crees or Cree-Assiniboins did not have a permanent home in Montana until they, along with numerous mixed-bloods, managed to get themselves on the final role of the reservation established in 1916 for Rocky and his band of Chippewas and for other homeless Montana Indians. The phase "She was wild, from Rocky Boy" (2), used by the narrator to describe the woman over whom he got into a fight at the beginning of the novel, would be self explanatory to a Montana reservation Indian. Agnes, as a Cree from nearby Havre, "scorned by reservation people" (4), inherited the reputation of her people. See John Ewers, *Ethnological Report on the Chippewa Cree Tribe of the Rocky Boy Reservation, Montana, and the Little Shell Band of Indians*, Chippewa Indians, American Indian Ethnohistory: Northcentral and Northeastern Indians, 6 (New York: Garland, 1974); Verne Dusenberry, *The Montana Cree: A Study in Religious Persistence*, Stockholm Studies in Comparative Religion, 3 (Upsalla:Almqvist and Wiksells, 1962); and David Mandelbaum, *The Plains Cree*, Anthropological Papers of the American Museum of Natural History, 37.2 (New York, 1940): pp. 176-78, 181-87.

[13] Wissler 7.1:8-9 and McClintock 184. However, John E. Ewers indicates that

for many girls, chastity was more an ideal than a reality. See *The Blackfeet: Raiders on the Northwestern Plains* (Norman: University of Oklahoma Press, 1958), p. 98.

[14] Cooper 16.2:17. A Blackfeet myth of the morning star links a survivor to the sun. A-pi-su-ahts or Early Riser is the only one of all the many children of the sun and the moon (Ko-ko-mik-e-is or Night Light) who is not killed by pelicans (Grinnell 258, 263).

[15] The wild-eyed cow is a mythic figure which trancends time, as do Bird, Yellow Calf, and the grandmother. Like the grandmother, she gives birth long after what would be normal for her species. Because the most desirable breeding period for cows is from approximately two to twelve years, a cow who had had a calf at eleven or twelve would be "old." Further, Welch's description of the spinster cow as "dry that year" (p. 106) indicates that she had already calved previous to Mose's accident twenty years before. She would be at least twenty-three at the time the calf the narrator is trying to wean was born. Although some cows reach twenty, most are disposed of long before this age. Because of the age issue, I had originally thought Welch was describing two different cows. However, I am now convinced that he is using the wild-eyed cow as a mythic figure.

Riding
the
Earthboy
40

Selections from
Riding the Earthboy 40

◆

MAGIC FOX

They shook the green leaves down,
those men that rattled
in their sleep. Truth became
a nightmare to their fox.
He turned their horses into fish,
or was it horses strung
like fish, or fish like fish
hung naked in the wind?

Stars fell upon their catch.
A girl, not yet twenty-four
but blonde as morning birds, began
a dance that drew the men in
green around her skirts.
In dust her magic jangled memories
of dawn, till fox and grief
turned nightmare in their sleep.

And this: fish not fish but stars
that fell into their dreams.

THE WORLD'S ONLY CORN PALACE

They came with knives and sticks—
no one called, no one reminded
the wild man of his right to scream,
to fall sobbing to his knees.
With sticks they came—this pack
so bent on killing all his bones.

Some looked away; others in their throats
began to laugh, not loud, but blue,
a winter blue that followed
mongrels out the door. With knives
those killers carved initials on his heart
till his eyes grew white with wonder.

Thunderbird came heavy on our heads.
Too much of a good thing
can spoil it for poets, you said.
I agreed. Down by the river we sang
sad tunes and O the stars
were bright that melancholy night.

RIDING THE EARTHBOY 40

Earthboy: so simple his name
should ring a bell for sinners.
Beneath the clowny hat, his eyes
so shot the children called him
dirt, Earthboy farmed this land
and farmed the sky with words.

The dirt is dead. Gone to seed
his rows become marker to a grave
vast as anything but dirt.
Bones should never tell a story
to a bad beginner. I ride
romantic to those words,

those foolish claims that he
was better than dirt, or rain
that bleached his cabin
white as bone. Scattered in the wind
Earthboy calls me from my dream:
Dirt is where the dreams must end.

THERE IS A RIGHT WAY

The justice of the prairie hawk
moved me; his wings tipped
the wind just right and the mouse
was any mouse. I came away,
broken from my standing spot,
dizzy with the sense of a world
trying to be right, and the mouse
a part of a wind that stirs the plains.

GRANDMA'S MAN

That day she threw the goose over the roof
of the cowshed, put her hand to her lips
and sucked, cursing, the world ended. In blood
her world ended though these past twenty years
have healed the bite and that silly goose
is preening in her favorite pillow.

Her husband was a fool. He laughed too long
at lies told by girls whose easy virtue disappeared
when he passed stumble-bum down the Sunday street.
Baled hay in his every forty, cows on his allotted range
his quick sorrel quarter-horse, all neglected for
the palms of friends. Then, he began to paint LIFE.

His first attempt was all about a goose that bit
the hand that fed it. The obstacles were great.
Insurmountable. His fingers were too thick to grip
the brush right. The sky was always green
and hay spoiled in the fields. In wind,
the rain, the superlative night, images came, geese
skimming to the reservoir. This old man listened.
He got a bigger brush and once painted the cry
of a goose so long, it floated off the canvas
into thin air. Things got better. Sky turned white.
Winter came and he became quite expert at snowflakes
But he was growing wise, Lord, his hair white as snow.

Funny, he used to say, how mountains are blue
in winter and green in spring. He never ever
got things quite right. He thought a lot about the day
the goose bit Grandma's hand. LIFE seldom came
the shade he wanted. Well, and yes, he died well,
but you should have seen how well his friends took it.

GOING TO REMAKE THIS WORLD

Morning and the snow might fall forever.
I keep busy. I watch the yellow dogs
chase creeping cars filled with Indians
on their way to the tribal office.
Grateful trees tickle the busy underside
of our snow-fat sky. My mind is right,
I think, and you will come today
for sure, this day when the snow falls.

From my window, I see bundled Doris Horseman,
black in the blowing snow, her raving son,
Horace, too busy counting flakes to hide his face.
He doesn't know. He kicks my dog
and glares at me, too dumb to thank the men
who keep him on relief and his mama drunk.

My radio reminds me that Hawaii calls
every afternoon at two. Moose Jaw is overcast,
twelve below and blowing. Some people...
Listen: if you do not come this day, today
of all days, there is another time
when breeze is tropic and riffs the green sap
forever up these crooked cottonwoods.
    Sometime,
you know, the snow never falls forever.

THE ONLY BAR IN DIXON

These Indians once imitated life.
Whatever made them warm
they called wine, song or sleep,
a lucky number on the tribal roll.

Now the stores have gone the gray
of this November sky. Cars
whistle by, chrome wind, knowing
something lethal in the dust.

A man could build a reputation here.
Take that redhead at the bar—
she knows we're thugs, killers
on a fishing trip with luck.

No luck. No room for those
sensitive enough to know they're beat.
Even the Flathead turns away,
a river thick with bodies,

Indians on their way to Canada.
Take the redhead—yours for just a word,
a promise that the wind will warm
and all the saints come back for laughs.

SURVIVING

The day-long cold hard rain drove
like sun through all the cedar sky
we had that late fall. We huddled
close as cows before the bellied stove.
Told stories. Blackbird cleared his mind,
thought of things he'd left behind, spoke:

"Oftentimes, when sun was easy in my bones,
I dreamed of ways to make this land."
We envied eagles easy in their range.
"That thin girl, old cook's kid, stripped naked
for a coke or two and cooked her special stew
round back of the mess tent Sundays."
Sparrows skittered through the black brush.

That night the moon slipped a notch, hung
black for just a second, just long enough
for wet black things to sneak away our cache
of meat. To stay alive this way, it's hard...

GRAVELY

we watched her go the way she came,
unenvied, wild—cold as last spring rain.
Mule deer browsed her garden down
to labored earth, seed and clean carrots.

Dusk is never easy, yet she took it
like her plastic saint, grandly, the day
we cut those morning glories down
and divvied up her odds and ends.

Daughters burned sheets the following Monday.
All over God's city, the high white stars
welcomed her the way she'd planned: a chilly
satellite ringing round the great malicious moon.

GRANDFATHER AT THE
REST HOME

I am standing high and frail.
Worms are breathing in my bones.
My eyes are cataracts
and dams back up my blood.
The birds are singing chirps,
chirps go in my ears.
I am drowning.

I should have known you would come
today, the birds sing
in my bones. Stranger to me now,
your words go through the grass
like snakes. My appetite is pure
for the quick sweet taste of apples.

Apples, here come the apples.
That bulgy, baggy brown sack
you carry in your skin
is filled with apples.

Apples for me now,
apples for the king!

Oh, that murderous, knifing waltz
we counted on so many years ago
is going, gone, the price the keen apples.
My blood sings the birds farewell.

Blackfeet Winter Blues

◆

Kenneth Lincoln

They shook the green leaves down,
those men that rattled
in their sleep. Truth became
a nightmare to their fox.

He turned their horses into fish,
or was it horses strung
like fish, or fish like fish
hung naked in the wind?

Stars fell upon their catch.
A girl, not yet twenty-four
but blonde as morning birds, began
 a dance that drew the men in
green around her skirts.
In dust her magic jangled memories
of dawn, till fox and grief
turned nightmare in their sleep.

And this: fish not fish but stars
that fell into their dreams.

This poem, "Magic Fox," opens *Riding the Earthboy 40* (1971), Welch's
collected poetry, in a dreamed reality that cannot settle between
likenesses and things in themselves. Truth is a fox's game refusing to

make sense. To "ride" a plot of earth implies a precarious stability from the start. "And the rolling day,/it will never stop? It means nothing?" Welch asks in "Getting Things Straight." The poet's shamanic mystery comes under question: truth turns to nightmarish magic, love swirls with nervous leaves in a dance of memories, and poetry shifts on a dangerously unstable set of images. The traditional death chant, to meet the rattling darkness, has been transformed into the sounds of elderly men snoring leaves off the sun dance tree of life. Even the Trickster's cousin, fox, Welch's quick-witted totem (later paired with the wheeling hawk, a symbol of the circling needs of hunger and the hunt), is not sharp-eyed or sharp-clawed enough to unravel what is here the unreality of reality. There are no fixed points: all is in disquiet, falling. Trickster has doubled back on himself with a self-defeating wit.

We know that the stars did slip and fall in a nineteenth-century nightmare sky. Following the 1833 Leonid meteor showers, smallpox killed two thirds of the 20,000 Blackfeet in 1837, and there were successive plagues in 1845, 1857, and 1869 (Ewers, pp.65-66; Curtis, p. 6). The horses were shot by cavalry or led away like so many bagged fish on a string (as the buffalo were slaughtered and reservations staked). The sacred sun dance tree was torn down, to be replaced by the cross and the flagpole. And the poet-shaman, haunted by nightmares of a past that skews the present, is now discredited, with a "blonde" memory of his people's seduction and fall. He wakes to the dangers of a shamanic medicine that failed, the instability of magic and metaphor, remembering that in the old days a medicine man who failed could be ostracized or even killed. The "all-face man," as the Blackfeet shaman was known, can find no tribal mask now, no patronage among his people, and his power goes underground, a "holy ghost" questioning itself along "Arizona Highways," or lost in the alcoholic antiways of "Blue Like Death":

> You see, the problem is
> no more for the road . . .
> the way is not your going
> but an end. That road awaits
> the moon that falls between
> the snow and you, your stalking home.

The Blackfeet poet's voice descends from the shaman's tongue, mysterious and ritualistic, chanting "finicky secrets" like a nighthawk, in strange, concentrated phases, in paradox and parable; his images seem refracted from ordinary associations, as a nightmare is filtered through the dark side of day-to-day life. His words, as in "Counting Clouds," are difficult, contrary:

> a long way to come—
> this rain so old my bones
> crackle no before you speak.
> A way to come: downwind
> before the sudden clouds appear,
> turn you statue—no, I say,
> no to the north and no, no
> to your crummy mirror.

Grinnel notes (p. 284) that a medicine doctor for the Blackfeet was literally "a heavy singer for the sick." His terribly familiar voice cast insights into the shadows of people's lives, as the poet-shaman says of the nighthawk's secrets, "And another: man is afraid of his dark." Fear feeds a shaman's power; he teaches how to live with the unknown and uncontrollable, how to use the threatening world as a source of courage. In a traditional song-poem, a Pima sings,

> There I run in rattling darkness
> cactus flowers in my hair
> in rattling darkness
>   darkness rattling
> running to that singing place (Brandon, p. 37)

Along with courage born of fear, the poet-shaman also knows the alembic of anger. In "The Versatile Historian" Welch calls out for "mountains to bang against," a rhythm that rages everywhere among images. In "Surviving" he remembers,

> The day-long cold hard rain drove
> like sun through all the cedar sky
> we had that late fall. We huddled
> close as cows before the bellied stove.

Just as the old warrior songs moved the tribe into battle, the new poem, "In My Lifetime," drums the people to arms against the self-defeat of acculturated poverty:

> With thunder—
> hands his father shaped the dust, circled
> fire, tumbled up the wind to make a fool.
> Now the fool is dead. His bones go back
> so scarred in time, the buttes are young to look
> for signs that say a man could love his fate,
> that winter in the blood is one sad thing.
>
> His sins—I don't explain. Desperate in my song,
> I run these woman hills, translate wind
> to mean a kind of life, the children of Speakthunder
> are never wrong and I am rhythm to strong medicine.

Na'pi may have created man-the-fool in his own image, ironically, while Thunder gave the tribe a medicine bundle to pray for saving rain: the bundle is still opened each spring after the first thunder is heard (Ewers, p. 172). A contemporary Blackfeet, "blood to bison" and "desperate in my song," Welch inherits the original speech of Thunder in the poem, "In My Lifetime" (see, too, the end of Eliot's *Waste Land* where the thunder speaks a first language). The poet drinks wind of the sacred run after wild game, chants the old earth rhythms, drums the sky for rain, and translates breath into the rhymes of poetry. His rites of passage carry the running meter of Speakthunder into the crafted meters of a shamanic poet's vision quest. "Toward Dawn" opens with these words: "Today I search for a name." And in "Getting Things Straight" the lamenter in his quest asks the traditional four questions of the "circling" hawk: Is hunger the life need? Who feeds the hawk? Am I his prey? Is he my vision? Riding toward "Crystal" in a night of drunken insight, when horses begin to sing, coyotes prowl in the blooming moonlight, and places mean their names, the poet does not so much "try to understand" as to witness "Crystal's gray dawn."

Traditional Indian verse ritualized the relationships between things through the use of corresponding ideas and objects. In contrast to the parallel phrasing of old chant formulas, Welch clusters images discordantly, using internal rhyme and rhythm to hold lines together. In "Counting Clouds" the poet couples the eidetic imagery and spiritual tension of surrealism, distantly related to the vision quest, with a Blackfeet attention to the land and the people:

> Once I loved this gravy land
> so famous in my blood
> my hair turned black
> with love. A way to think:
> so cold the sun could call me
> friend.

This palimpsest of modern style and Indian tradition is paralleled in the visual art of Oscar Howe, a Lakota painter who fuses the hallucinatory energy of Indian visions with cubist forms (see in particular *Medicine Man* and *Dakota Eagle Dancer*, 1962). Under intense compression, disquiet between old and new forms stirs the reader's sense of involvement; ideas call to a receding past, attempt rhyme, and grope for clarity. The poems impact as surreal conversations, densely imagistic, that follow structured stutters of the mind. An image suspends thought in midair; an ellipsis, colon, or hyphen trails an idea beyond recorded speech; a full-stop jolts the rhythm to halt in midline, as in "Going to Remake This World":

> Moose Jaw is overcast,
> twelve below and blowing. Some people . . .
> Listen: if you do not come this day, today
> of all days, there is another time
> when breeze is tropic and riffs the green sap
> forever up these crooked cottonwoods.
> Sometimes,
> you know, the snow never falls forever.

Welch writes a poetry of startling half-lines and broken forms (not unlike John Berryman's *Dream Songs*). Conversational syntax and diction tense against formal line lengths, so that verses enjamb or break at midpoint; fragments of images splinter in commonplace rhythms, broken lines of thought, and abrupt full stops. And within lines ideas implode in rhyme: "Look away and we are gone./Look back. Tracks are there . . ." Beginning with the idea that Fox could be related to Native American Trickster figures such as Coyote (but Fox is more a European import than a traditional Indian trickster), Welch explores the possibilities of near-rhyme crisscross in the words "dance" and "fox" and "catch" and "fish" in "Magic Fox," and carries the method through as a unifying technique to the closing poem, "Never Give a Bum an Even Break": "—instead he *spoke/* of a role so *black* the *uncle* died/ out of *luck* in a westend *shack* " (italics mine). The near rhymes and sharp repetitions of explosive sounds, a forced yoking of old and new ways, remind us of "a woman blue as night" stepping from the medicine bundle and singing of a slant-rhyming world "like this far off" in "Verifying the Dead," the old ways gone but echoed on in Blackfeet blues:

> Have mercy on me, Lord. Really. If I should die
> before I wake, take me to that place I just heard
> banging in my ears. Don't ask me. Let me join
> the other kings, the ones who trade their knives
> for a sack of keys. Let me open any door,
> stand winter still and drown in a common dream.

This ironically assimilated "Lord's Prayer" in "Dreaming Winter" jars against the older Blackfeet belief that the shadows of souls go to rest in the "Sand Hills" on the Saskatchewan border (Grinnell, p. 273).The old stories scatter as shards of ancient earthenware. Welch recalls in "Blackfeet, Blood and Piegan Hunters":

> We ended sometime
> back in recollections of glory, myths
> that meant the hunters meant a lot
> to starving wives and bad painters.
>
> Let glory go the way of all sad things.

The fall of Icarus appears as a sign to the drunken Indian who envisions "his future falling" in "Two for the Festival." The poet comes stumbling on "awkward rhymes" cradling a blind toad (the "all-face" toad was associated with a medicine man whose coiled hair likened him to a horned toad), the magic fox and his surreal truth, and "thirteen lumpy stones" (a reduction of the sacred "buffalo stones," once powerful hunting medicine). All this medicine power—totems, beasts, myths, chants—in no way prevents the fall of either Icarus or the Indian. Fox hugs his stones in fear. One more drink and the drunk goes home, dreaming of middle-class Christian keys to heaven, of a salvation that has nothing to do with neolithic knives and bones. Welch mocks the Indian's fantasy of possessing New World riches, of opening "any door," of standing "winter still" in white American prosperity and drowning "in a common dream" of melting-pot, self-help democracy. In "Harlem, Montana: Just Off the Reservation,"

> Booze is law
> and all the Indians drink in the best tavern.
> Money is free if you're poor enough
> Disgusted, busted whites are running
> for office in this town.

Deafy, the silent cigar-store stereotype, can't hear the world anymore behind his "drum-tight ear," so he pretends he's "dumb" in "There Are Silent Legends":

> Though wind has shut his ears for good, he squats
> for hours at the slough, skipping stones, dreaming
> of a moon, the quiet nights and a not quite done
> love with a lady high in costly red shoes.

Bleeding from a smile, nose smashed straight and teeth scrubbed away with stones, wearing the mask of American camaraderie, the "civilized" savage acquiesces, head down, penitent, and "happy for the snow clean hands of you, my friends" in "Plea to Those Who Matter." And, back on the reservation, unregenerate Indians are "Surviving":

> The night the moon slipped a notch, hung
> black for just a second, just long enough
> for wet black things to sneak away our cache
> of meat. To stay alive this way, it's hard . . .

Though self-wounded by these double-edged ironies, Welch counters the American myth of White plenty by giving thanks for Blackfeet seasons of loss, a mind of late fall and winter. The "noble savage" in "Directions to the Nomad" "instructs stars,/but only to the thinnest wolf." And "In My First Hard Springtime" the poet challenges:

> Starved to visions, famous cronies top Mount Chief
> for names to give respect to Blackfeet streets.
> I could deny them in my first hard springtime,
> but choose amazed to ride you down with hunger.

An essential paradox of Indian ritual (and now, inversely, of tribal history in America) lies in an old concept of *humilitas*, the power of loss.[1] "Pity me," the sun dancers cry in flesh-piercing ceremonies; the vision seekers chant "Listen" to the spirits. In Indian traditions the ritual loss of self brings spiritual gain, as winter warms the blood, hunger sharpens the eye, and the lonely vision quest leads the dreamer back into the tribe. So in "Thanksgiving at Snake Butte" the Indians ride to the crest of a holy mountain and find petroglyphs left crudely, without pretense, by their wandering ancestors, "driven by their names/ for time":

> On top, our horses broke, loped through
> a small stand of stunted pine, then jolted
> to a nervous walk. Before us lay
> the smooth stones of our ancestors, the fish,
> the lizard, snake and bent-kneed
> bowman—etched by something crude,
> by a wandering race, driven by their names
> for time: its winds, its rain, its snow
> and the cold moon tugging at the crude figures
> in this, the season of their loss.

The old ones lived out their names, imaged the needs of their seasonal losses, hunted for their lives, and depended on the animal in themselves to know when more is less under a "snow-fat sky." Bowed in rituals of blood sacrifice, "bent-kneed" bowman climbed lonely buttes to lose themselves into their world's uncompromising truths. Thanksgiving, then, cuts two ways at once like a double-edged knife: the seasonal and positive ritual loss in the old ways of finding strength in abstinence, designed to meet necessity; and the historical, cultural loss ensuing from the first Algonquians giving thanks with the Pilgrims in 1621. Algonquian speakers who migrated westward before the invasion, the Blackfeet were at odds with the "Big Knives" from their first encounter on the plains. "No one spoke of our good side,/those times we fed the hulking idiot,/mapped these plains with sticks/and flint," Welch recalls in "The Renegade Wants Words." During a "quick 30 below" blizzard in "Christmas Comes to Moccasin Flat":

> Christmas comes like this: Wise men
> unhurried, candles bought on credit (poor price
> for calves), warriors face down in wine sleep.
> Winds cheat to pull heat from smoke.

Blackfeet children beg for legends, "a myth that tells them be alive," and Medicine Woman, spitting at her television to predict the end of day by the five o'clock news, translates the old Christian and Indian stories: "a peculiar evening star" bringing light to people in need, "something about honor and passion,/warriors back with meat and song." The original Savior (the Ghost Dancers of the late 1880s imagined an Indian Christ returning) perhaps appears more mythically alive to "warriors face down in wine," hungry friends awaiting supplies, children leaning into a grandmother's stale breath, and Charlie Blackbird feeding his fire against the dark cold of winter. In the late 1880s Ghost Dancers joined hands, danced in circles, and chanted until they fell down in visions:

> The whirlwind! The whirlwind!
>
> The new earth comes into being
> swiftly as snow.
>
> The new earth comes into being
> quietly as snow.[2]

In "Legends like This" Welch sees the crucified Savior as a renegade poet flanked by two other hostiles, "dying in the sight of God," who never bothered to learn their true names. Resurrected as renegade poets of the lost tribe, they "burned His church/and hid out for a long, long time."

The interwoven Christian, Indian, and Homeric fragments of myth, then, seem archaic dreams of the past, broken relics for exiles who suffer the losses of the present. In "Spring for All Seasons" the poet sees that "Our past is ritual,/cattle marching one way to remembered mud." The narrator at the end of *Winter in the Blood* recalls: "Somewhere in my mind I could hear the deep rumble of thunder, or maybe it was the rumble of energy, the rumble of guts—it didn't matter. There was only me, a white horse and a cow" (*WB*, p. 191). Not questioning the source—signaled by the voice of spring thunder, or animal flatulence—Welch's Blackfeet carry on, surviving the present.

The old Blackfeet ways taught the people how to survive in a severe northern climate, how to grow stronger in seasons of loss. Accurate translations of these ways in poetry and prose guide modern Native Americans through an imposed winter of white culture and steel them against the "sentimental crap" of country and western songs in junction bars.

The pain of truth opens the people's eyes in "The World's Only Corn Palace":

> Some looked away; others in their throats
> began to laugh, not loud, but blue,
> a winter blue that followed
> mongrels out the door. With knives
> those killers carved initials on his heart
> till his eyes grew white with wonder.

The last section of *Riding the Earthboy 40*, "The Day the Children Took Over," tempers the hand-to-hand struggles of the opening "Knives" section, pulls back from the "renegade" bitterness of the second section, and moves beyond the third section's image of a poet weaving styptic spider webs (the old medicine for wounds) "to bandage up the day" in "Snow Country Weavers." With winter in their blood the children redefine a season of cold beauty "in their own image," as a time of counterplay "to create life." A psychic cultural storm locks conventional mothers, lovers, statesmen, and priests in the arms of their losses.[3] These closing poems register a spirit of reconciliation and defiant reaffirmation—the warrior's serious play with the odds against his people. Militants, like Montana weathers, move the tribe against white assimilation in "Call to Arms": "The eyes were with us,/every one, and we were with the storm." Instead of retreating into the sentiment of defeat, "cattle marching one way to remembered mud," Welch brings a warrior's courage forward, under pressure of necessity, to battle against coercion from mainstream America: "None looked behind,/but heard the mindless suck of savage booted feet." And "Gravely" the old ones die: "we watched her go the way she came,/unenvied, wild—cold as last spring rain."

Na'pi's mask reappears in the final poem, "Never Give a Bum an Even Break," a title borrowed from W. C. Fields. If Thunder gave the original medicine bundle to invoke spring rain for the Blackfeet, Welch's bundle of chants opens in the "fall" of Indian time and finally drums up a spring "comic rain" to thaw the grip of winter (see also the regenerative "comic" rain at the end of *Winter in the Blood*). Resistant to White society, the poet still is hostile—leaving middle-class mirrors and waiting with a fellow bum to blow up "one of the oldest bridges in town," perhaps an underground bridge of extended kinship to the "other side," severing the illusory goodwill tie between Red and White cultures.[4] The old scores of history must be settled—the broken treaties, the land stolen by "a slouching dwarf with rainwater eyes," the present poverty and despair, the condescending acculturation policies, the termination threats—or Indians must create new roles, as the poet adapts to a changing world by shifting to new forms of tribal medicine. The emergent roles may transcend a history of grief and anger. But, for now, the "all-face" poet remains the contemporary shaman, the warrior, the vision seeker in a White freezing desert, chanting his angers, nightmares, laments, and conflicts as verbal "masks/glittering in a comic rain." This is Welch's Native American art, purged of losses, regenerating, reintegrating in the world as it is:

> We are the sovereign and free children of Mother Earth. Since before human memory our people have lived on this land. For countless generations, we have lived in harmony with our relatives, the four-leggeds, the winged beings, the beings that swim, and the beings that crawl. For all time our home is from coast to coast, from pole to pole.
>
> We are the original people of this hemisphere. The remains of our ancestors and of our many relatives are

a greater part of this land than any others' remains. The mountains and the trees are a part of us. We are the human beings of many nations, and we still speak many tongues. We have come from the four directions of this Turtle Island. We are the evidence of the Western Hemisphere, the carriers of the original ways of this area of the world, and the protectors of all life on this earth.

Today we address you in the language of the oppressor, but the concepts predate the coming of the invaders. The injustice we speak of is centuries old. We have spoken against it in our many tongues. We are still the origianl people of this land. We are the people of *The Longest Walk.* [5]

Notes

---

[1]See Dennis and Barbara Tedlock, eds., *Teachings from the American Earth: Indian Religion and Philosophy* (New York: Liveright, 1975).

[2]William Brandon, ed., *The Magic World: American Indian Songs and Poems* (New York: Morrow, 1971), p. 129.

[3]John C. Ewers, *The Blackfeet: Raiders of the Northwest Plains* (Norman: University of Oklahoma Press, 1958). Chapter Eight, "All in Fun," describes the traditional Blackfeet winter sports such as sliding and sledding, ice tops, and blanket tossing games.

[4]See, in particular, the anthropologist's identification as an extended kin with "neolithic" cultures in Claude Le'vi-Strauss' *Tristes Tropiques* and the Savage Mind.

[5]*Wassaja*, 6, Nos. 7-8 (Aug.-Sept. 1978), 9-10. The statement begins an address to the United States Congress in 1977 made by the tribal coalition of traditional elders on the Longest Walk. To protest the abrogation of treaties the people reversed Manifest Destiny by walking for half a year from the West Coast to the East Coast.

Almost Not on the Map

———————————◆———————————

Peter Wild

For an Anglo to go native, to take up the ways of an American Indian tribe, and then write poetry from the Anglo perspective in his adopted language would seem absurdly precious to most of us. It certainly would to most Indians. For one thing, traditional Native American poetry has a far different purpose than our lyrics, which pique the esthetic sensibilities of readers, while, often, venting the weltschmerz of their writers. For another, a traditional Indian culture has no "reading audience" for poetry as Anglos conceptualize it. Poetry exists to serve practical ends. It heals the sick and assures success in hunting.

Yet, going the other way, this is precisely the reversal that a Native American poet goes through if he is to get a hearing in a predominantly English-speaking country. For anyone, writing poetry is a hazardous undertaking at best. For a person from an "ethnic" group, then, the hazards are more numerous and greater. With this in mind, it is not surprising that many an Indian poet has easily slid into the trap our society generously sets before him:asking for, not individual vision, but for the repetition of cliches and the social angst and anger that we think should be the Native American's foremost concerns. Anglos seem to find this satisfying, and for his part why shouldn't the Indian do the old dance that wins him ready applause?

That poet James Welch for the most part has refused to go for the bait is much to his credit. Early in his career he declared that he wanted to be a poet first, not an ethnic poet. To keep up the illusion of independence, many a writer has voiced that claim, but few have had the fortitude to follow through on it. James Welch has contributed a strong element in making his poetry enduring rather than frivolous.

But it takes more than fortitude to be a good poet. It takes a combination of qualities—one perhaps ultimately inenarrable but nonetheless readily recognizable—of wholeness, of being able to synthesize what we as readers perceive as daily events into unusual perspectives. They leave us esthetically refreshed and surprised, leave us seeing more in existence than we did the moment before we penetrated the poem. The best poems of James Welch have that quality, whatever the name it goes by.

Perhaps it should be said at this point that this doesn't mean James Welch has "sold out," as we used to say in the 1960s. He has not become a "white Indian," to use a somewhat execrable term, in order to reap the benefits of the white man's world. Part Blackfeet, part Gros Ventre, he doesn't deny this rich aspect of his upbringing any more than he denies that he is a person from Montana with a decidedly rural and small-town background. All of which is to say, however, that he is wise enough to do what any good writer does: he turns the material of himself to his own best esthetic ends.

I have written elsewhere about James Welch's poems and the aspects that make them "work."[1] Suffice it to say here that when they come off at their peak, they show the humor, wit, *joie* of using language, and psychic penetration already alluded to. Working together, such aspects rush us magically to places we've never been before, places not on the map. To continue the metaphor in Blyian terms, at his best Welch's poetic sensibilities take his readers soaring over a heightened Montana landscape, looking down with him on a tavern in Dixon or on some old Indian taking up painting for a past time, botching the job but having a hell of a time doing it.

And Welch has written some near bummers, too—haven't we all? These happen, it seems to me, when he forces the issue, riding his horse with the spurs instead of the reins, taking it all too earnestly. He ends up substituting for his own clear vision the wooden imagery of bones, worms, and stars that at its worst and most wooden can be the poorer part of Wright's and Bly's legacy. In contrast, it also happens when Welch's sheer fun with words—ah, the ecstatic but necessary dangers of that!—take *him* for a ride, and off go horse and poet on a silly romp.

I want to turn now from both categories to one rarely considered with writers, those poems that nearly make it into the blue-ribbon class but fall short, that promise but don't deliver on their potential. They neither fly off, taking us breathless into the poetic ether, nor crash ignominiously at some little distance from where they were launched. Instead, they wobble off—touching ground here, squeaking over a housetop there—unsure of themselves into poetic limbo.

Goodness knows, any poet worth the name writes his share of these as well as the bummers—so this is not meant as a detraction. And we cannot say precisely what went wrong in the process leading to the completed poem, why the intended horse turned out a camel—what promising whim-wham got jammed, what chemical keys failed to mesh in the laboring poet's head. What quotidian mailman came knocking on the door and threw over the whole poetic apple cart. But we do have the poems before us on the page, and whatever the unknown causes, we can talk about the results, the places in a piece where the hand jolts, the poem goes astray.

This can happen in various ways, of course, and to any poet. The poem can be wrong, stillborn from the beginning. For whatever reason, cosmic or not, this year or maybe for the next ten years the poet is not up to taking on the subject with which he insists on wrestling. Or it could be the glint of a word on the page that leads him astray, into associations having no business being there, takes him off the main track of the poem and bouncing across the underbrush. Or it can be a question of the larger schema, a failure to fulfill the promised organization. The poem seems to be going along just fine toward a goal, a completion that we cannot yet see but with all certainty believe exists. But we don't arrive there. Prepared for a party at the shore, we end up in the mountains, abashed at our swimming trunks and beach balls.

Why even bother with such an analysis? one might ask parenthetically. Because it sharpens our sensibilities for poems in general, those of others and our own included. Because it shows us just how tough it is to get through the process of writing a good poem, one good all the way through. And because it increases our thrill for the ride when, careening around poetic blind curves at breakneck speed, we arrive—yes, at the beach—but at a beach party prepared for us more glorious than we—and probably the poet—ever imagined.

In any case, I'd like to suggest that Welch's "Going To Remake The

World"[2] belongs in the third category mentioned above. In many ways, it is a workmanlike, if not outstanding, job, having the "right" instincts, doing many of the "right" things a poem should do. Yet in the final analysis one is left with the feeling that as is the poem has not filled out its promise, is not yet complete, that the final stanza is false.

One could spend some time singing Welch's praises in the first stanza:

> Morning and the snow might fall forever.
> I keep busy. I watch the yellow dogs
> chase creeping cars filled with Indians
> on their way to the tribal office.
> Grateful trees tickle the busy underside
> of our snow-fat sky. My mind is right,
> I think, and you will come today
> for sure, this day when the snow falls.

Importantly, so that we can gain our poetic bearings, Welch sets the scene, lets us know where we are. He disarms us. Using straighforward language, he invites us into the world of the poem, the world of a small Montana town populated in winter by yellow dogs and creeping cars. His rendition seems just right.

But of course, no poet's world is as simple as that. The simplicity is an illusion, a trick to make us feel comfortable while the poet works his magic. Slowly, subtly, Welch drops hints that things are not as they seem. In the midst of this supposedly peaceful scene, the poet is watchful, waiting, an outsider. Through his eyes, we see a world changed. The trees are grateful, the sky fat. What's going on? Well, the "I" has been having problems. Playfully echoing a line in Robert Lowell's "Skunk Hour,"[3] a poem about Lowell's madness, the "I" tells us that his mind is doing just fine, then undercuts this with the conditional. So grows Welch's tone, one of patient anxiety, of anticipation, set off against the ordinary town life and clothed in a whimsical, bittersweet humor. One that, furthermore, prepares us for the developing complexity, that makes us as readers anxious for what will happen, for where the poem is taking us. Note, in this respect, that Welch somewhat casually throws in the "you," whetting our curiosity.

But he veers away from that and in the second stanza zooms in on a specific scene. It shows us what life is like on the streets of the little town:

From my window, I see bundled Doris Horseman,
black in the blowing snow, her raving son,
Horace, too busy counting flakes to hide his face.
He doesn't know. He kicks my dog
and glares at me, too dumb to thank the men
who keep him on relief and his mama drunk.

So that's Doris Horseman and her son in a vignette of mixed
violence, pity, and humor. Things are getting worse, both for the
observer and the world observed. Against the backdrop of a benign
nature, people aren't doing too well. As Lowell says metaphorically in
his poem, "The season's ill." So to be suffering the mental shakes as the
"I" is in Welch's poem is one thing. To be suffering them in a world
already gone over the brink makes the "I"'s condition all the worse.
The situation holds out little promise of restored health.

The plot thickens, our anxiety builds. How is the poet going to
resolve the seemingly irresolvable situation he's created?

He has an ace up his sleeve, the "you" mentioned in stanza one, not
entirely forgotten by us as a figure standing in the poem's wings. Who
or what the "you" is we don't know. Perhaps a friend or a girlfriend
who can smooth the mental waters and make things seem right.
Perhaps the poet's inspiration personified, the inspiration that can, at
least in a poem, impose order on chaos. So the final stanza:

My radio reminds me that Hawaii calls
every afternoon at two. Moose Jaw is overcast,
twelve below and blowing. Some people . . .
Listen: if you do not come this day, today
of all days, there is another time
when breeze is tropic and riffs the green sap
forever up these crooked cottonwoods.
        Sometimes,
you know, the snow never falls forever.

There's some fine writing here, but technically it's the weakest
stanza, and that's all the worse since it's the conclusion. We don't need,
for instance, the obvious irony of the first sentence. By now, we're
wound up for the finale, for the rabbit to come out of the hat, and the
reference to Hawaii, to a world outside the poem, shatters rather than
strengthens Welch's setup. In places the language itself becomes

troublesome: "when breeze is tropic" may be an ironic echo of travel-brochure promises, but it's unpleasing to the ear, jolting when we don't need to be jolted. And it's smarty-pants.

That the "I" in the poem is even more confused than when we met him in stanza one is understandable. But note the above in conjunction with the abrupt but unresolved shifts in the middle of stanza three. They indicate that the writer himself, the controller of the poem, also is confused, and this undermines our confidence, our trust that he can control his material and bring the poem off.

And the "you" doesn't appear. This in itself is not the problem. On the one hand, we can't expect friend or genie to emerge magically just at the most intense moment of crisis and make everthing hunky-dory. It could be farcical if such a figure did pop out and—kazaaam!—cure the "I" 's pain.

The problem, then, is not the nonappearance of the "you," but the poet's handling of it. And though the last line is especially *jejune*, the apparent message of the entire last stanza seems to be, "Ah, well. Things are tough, but tomorrow is another day." We are left unsatisfied with that nostrum, that failure to come to grips with the situation established, all the more so because in the endings of his better pieces Welch deftly drops in the unexpected catalysts that make the poems rush together into surprising wholes.

At the Only Bar in Dixon

$\blacklozenge$

Kim Stafford

What does it take to have a good time? Especially now, at August midnight, the only bar in Dixon is a warm light for Montana mosquito souls. Six of us hunch inward toward a story told by Elaine, the redhead in her laughing fifties at the bar:

> Yeah, Indians. Well, you know Mike Dubois. He comes
> in one time we're having this big party. He shows up
> holding a blue helium balloon on a string—thought
> that's how you have a good time, I guess. So I says to
> Don here, "See that guy down there, that Mike? He's
> Indian, and he's your cousin. You go down and intro-
> duce yourself." So Don goes down there, says, "Hey, I
> hear you're my cousin. Are you a Dubois?"
> "No," says Mike, "I'm a Kutenai."
> Can you believe that? "No, I'm Kutenai." So he went
> out with his balloon, went off drifting down the street.

Don sets down the glass he's been polishing and leans laughing on his arms. Some stories are good for a lifetime.

In the ripple of laughter along the bar, a sentence from James Welch's poem, "The Only Bar in Dixon," numbs my head: "These Indians once imitated life." If I were Kutenai here, if I were Flathead, Blackfeet, Gros Ventre, where would I let my gaze rest now? The

113

styrofoam cup in my hands? The bottle of Lewis & Clark Vodka on the counter where Don leans back? The plaque Elaine changes every week: "Town Drunk of the Week," with a slot for a hand-written name? The black velvet cradleboard above the cash register, with tufts of rabbitfur wrapping its peeled willow dream-shade? The match flame spitting from Don's hand as he lights his mother's cigarette?

"Hey, Elaine! When you going to wean that kid?"

◆

At the top of Lolo Pass on my way here, I stopped to read "The Only Bar in Dixon" by the day's last light:

> These Indians once imitated life.
> Whatever made them warm
> they called wine, song or sleep,
> a lucky number on the tribal roll.

Something caught my eye, and I looked up past the page at the dark hill of pines. Way off, a pillar of flame shot up. A forest fire? Too tall for a controlled burn.

> Now the stores have gone the gray
> of this November sky. Cars
> whistle by, chrome wind, knowing
> something lethal in the dust.

I looked up again. The distant flame wavered in place, slender and tall. A voice in my head said I should report it. I should throw the car into gear and race to the ranger station where my brother worked once, and pound on the door with my fist. A car whistled by.

> A man could build a reputation here.
> Take that redhead at the bar—
> she knows we're thugs, killers
> on a fishing trip with luck.

The sky darkened and the flame was brighter. A reputation for what?

No luck. No room for those
sensitive enough to know they're beat.

Something in what I had been reading made me want to address the
flame in a whisper. Not to report it but to speak to it: "They got
Geronimo, they got Joseph. You got away, traveling spirit, mouth
without a face."

Even the Flathead turns away,
a river thick with bodies,
Indians on their way to Canada.

My eyes had to strain to read. It was easier to look at the flame, a stem
of light swaying like a tree in wind.

Take the redhead—yours for just a word,
a promise that the wind will warm
and all the saints come back for laughs.

On the mountain I closed the book, and suddenly it's midnight and
everyone in the bar is laughing again. We're having a good time. It's
easy. It's something about Don being second in the state in high school.
Discus. Fifteen years ago. Pool balls crackle on felt behind me. Elaine
has launched into another story, but this time I can't hear more than a
few words. Colombo in a gray coat gestures toward a ship on the TV
screen no one watches. The cash register jangles, and Don is laughing
as he counts out change.

Fifteen years. That must have been about when Welch came here
with Richard Hugo and J. D. Reed, fishing for poems. In the *New
Yorker*, October 10, 1970, each had a poem called "The Only Bar in
Dixon." To read those three was to wish I had been there then. Hugo:
"Home. Home. I knew it entering." Reed: "For sale in the bar: a
shotgun, an electric guitar, / . . . ten minutes' warmth." Welch: "Even
the Flathead turns away." As often in Welch's poetry, there is a
confusion that illuminates. In one line, "the Flathead" seems to be an
Indian; in the next line, no, it is a river; in the next line, a river filled
with Indians. Human identity intrudes into the landscape and the
landscape turns with a human gesture. "Are you a Dubois?" "No.
Kutenai." And the regulars in the Dixon Bar laugh because that
answer is so hard to grasp.

What's wrong with being a dreamer? Why do so many Welch poems report a dream turning to steam in the hard light of our times, a dreamer's defeat? In the title poem of *Riding the Earthboy 40*, the man named Earthboy wore a clowny hat, and "farmed the sky with words." He is foolish and he dies: "Dirt is where the dreams must end." Yet the voice of Earthboy says this—Earthboy dead, scattered, wind. A dreamer's authority calls for the end of dreaming.

Down east from Lolo Pass, late in the evening on my way to Dixon, I stopped at a gas station arcade to call James Welch, to ask about how Earthboy came to be in the poem and the first novel both. The movement from poem to novel seemed to pivot on the half-presence of Earthboy.

To the raucous tune of pinball, I strained to follow Welch's congenial voice. I cupped my hand around the phone. A truck's headlights swept across me, and gunfire erupted from the video screen to my right.

"Earthboy was originally a long, lyrical poem in several parts," Welch said. "I went over the whole manuscript (for *Riding the Earthboy 40*) with my editor, and he convinced me to take that poem out. There wasn't any real drama to it. It was more a celebration of this family—the Earthboy family. They were our neighbors and we leased forty acres from them when I was a kid. So there I was with the title poem of the book gone. It's the only time I've done this, but I made a poem to fit that title—got some of that longer piece down to the bare bones.".

I expressed an interest in seeing the original version, the "long, lyrical poem," and then the revved engine of a truck drowned my thanks and farewell.

In that original manuscript version, too long for the book's editor, too full of the world's detail, there is a working knowledge of winter in the blood:

Riding the Earthboy 40

1.

These dog-tired days climbing
back through years wailing in my brain—
I don't accept. I fall through spring,

blind, more ancient than I should know.
Snow on ditch banks and this cabin,
once known to Earthboy, abandoned by some wife
in times of great depression, breaks my stare
that joins field to sky. I see magpies
fall light-boned down through willows
brittle in the wind. In sun, I shouldn't mind
this place—the garden grown with weeds,
sun, alive, a place I shouldn't mind to die.
Cottonwoods drum the sky. This crazy horse
hears and spooks, his off-white rump shivering
through weeds that hide a creek that never came.
Listening, I imagine birth crude, stupid,
practical when gods need time to die.
Because he believed he owned this land,
Earthboy built this shack of logs and mud,
took a wife from Lodgepole and settled into time.
His wife was strong, weathered those years of love
and came out hate. My grandmother called her
Cree and Crees are never any good.
These days are climbing in my brain.
I rode this way to cut years of river
from my age. The song of life is wind. My horse
hears, spook to quick brush, rattle and home—
rain-white mud, tired logs, the tin cup rusted,
wired to the tired pump. Sad faces on the graves
were carved by knives that hid a simpler instinct.
                    Denied my right to die,
I expect my bones to run the plains like half-crazed
buffalo before the jump, before a final impact
tells them it is final, a time for celebration.
My hands, married in guts of deer I killed,
on thighs steaming still before the cut throat,
deny a thought to win this land with song and wine,
with dance and magic of back-hill savvy.
Right to fail is a solitary thing.
The leather thongs are harsh to me; the lodgepole,
once upright, fantasy in wind.

2.

Ask a coyote child his name before the pain.
He builds his medicine around your words.
He says the trees are names and sun
no longer corners 'round the day.
My song, I say we speak
of nights that drain our lives
of winter wind and ice and dead men
we alone have pulled from rivers. Do you
wish me dead? My eyes are circles of despair.
My brain is filled with hungry dogs.
This skin, older than my name, becomes ascetic
in the wind. I travel forests of wind schemes,
geese cry directionless in my bones.
My eyes are brooding for a nest. Drink me in,
wind, cull the reed from my stalking eye, deliver
sundown vast as games we play with wrinkled thongs.
My name—you call me Earthboy.
I am also Comes At Night.
I am Coyote, Yellow Robe, Bear
Who Wanders Through The Day.
My name crawls on hair legs, my eyes
bright, black as earth.
You could ask me is there time
to snug our robes over your indifferent bones,
time to meld with dust our song,
to greet the sky with ash
from our burning hands?
Deliver up your heads to Coyote; your wives
are silent in their wind-smooth graves.
Study them and leave me to my vision:
I am eagle, meat-poised, wobbling through the night
back to nest with instinct. I am Coyote
shedding hair to give four winds direction.
Deliver me, winds, I am your meat.

3.

Lover once to old man talk, I ride these days
for symbols of a past. Fog shawls this famous land,
spreads itself across my back. I should have liked
to sing of other, more ancient men
whose deeds were whispered by the bear,
whose spirits choose the paths I take.
Where air sags in the sloughs below,
cranes and mud-hens battle out their lives,
diving through the memories of old coyotes
who watched the last warrior starve himself.
Because he believed he owned this land, he built
a shack of logs and mud, took a wife
from Lodgepole and lost his name.
These days are climbing through my brain.

Over twice the length of any poem in the printed collection, this text has several elements found nowhere in the book. The first section is filled with details that will reappear in *Winter in the Blood*: the scene at the Earthboy cabin with its weeds and graves (see the novel's opening paragraph); the animosity between the Cree wife and the grandmother; the town of Lodgepole; the "light-boned" magpies. The whole sense of natural life that fills the novel—with its narrator constantly noticing insect, bird, fish, even saving a tadpole from death—is given fuller treatment here than elsewhere in the poetry. And the second section's voice of Earthboy himself is distinctive: a visionary with multiple identities, a voice fervent without irony.

Elsewhere in the poetry there is an undercutting of this voice, its dignity set aside before it can be accused. In the final version of "Riding the Earthboy 40," Earthboy's claims to be "better than dirt" are "foolish." And in "The Only Bar in Dixon," Indians don't live, or even imitate life; rather, they "once imitated life." In Earthboy's long voice here, we are closer to the "old man talk" of traditional life. We don't hear it so plainly again until we meet Yellow Calf in Chapter 18 of *Winter in the Blood*.

This long version, "Riding the Earthboy 40," is poised between the compact irony of the finished poems and the broader pace of the fiction that followed it. Earthboy is old, and he speaks for a culture his neighbors find exotic—two marks of weakness, but also of authority. The shorter version may be a better poem. The long version haunts me.

At the only bar in Dixon, the radio is bringing us a song from somewhere way out of Montana. I can't quite follow the words— something about what defeat can bring. Beside the cradleboard a sign hangs on the wall, a little scrap of pseudo-immigrant poetry: "Ve are too soon old/ and too late schmardt." To be a double outsider—old, and foreign—is to have a kind of authority that is easy to laugh at, hard to forget. That's why Elaine put it there.

When I walk out from the bar, climb into the car at one AM, and put my hand on the book called *Riding the Earthboy 40*, I remember a moment in January, back about fifteen years. I was on the bus coming into the central Oregon reservation town of Warm Springs. Hard winter light through the green bus window lit an open book in the hands of the skier ahead of me: Jack Kerouac's *Dharma Bums*. The boy had fit a plain paper cover over it. At the end of a day on Mt. Bachelor west of Bend, he would again unwrap his secret, and imitate life. I looked across the aisle at a darker boy about the same age, putting away a paperback called *The Incredible Magic of the American Indian*. He was getting off in Warm Springs.

Then I had touched my coat pocket, where a tiny edition of Dante's *Divine Comedy* was ready for my need, was my own medicine-bundle that made any landscape approachable, any human crisis something for which I hungered.

The small glow of Dixon dwindles into the rearview mirror—my hand on *Riding the Earthboy 40* south past Arlee, Lolo, Victor, Sula, Chief Joseph Pass. Tomorrow, Wisdom.

The Death
of
Jim Loney

from
The Death of Jim Loney

◆

Jim Loney didn't know how long he had been asleep, but when he awoke it was close to 4 A.M. Outside, the wind swirled and blew snow like grains of sand against the kitchen window. He looked down at his dog and his dog was looking up at him.

"How you doing, old man?"

Swipesy twisted his head.

"You don't even hear me, but I think you understand everything about life. And you know that you're a good old boy, don't you? Yes, you're a good old dog. You live clean and you never abuse yourself. You're an example to me, Swipesy. I just wish I was as smart as you. I used to be. I was as smart as anybody."

Swipesy sat up and pushed his nose against Loney's knee.

"That was before I realized I didn't know anything. Not one damn thing that was worth knowing. Do you understand that? Do I understand that?" Loney allowed himself a rueful smile that had nothing to do with the dog.

He petted Swipesy until the dog slumped back to the floor. Then the lamp on the table flickered and went out. Loney sat for a moment and listened to the wind. From the dark room he could see the sheet of snow blowing through the street lamp beside the Catholic church.

He stood and walked the five feet to the refrigerator. He felt around on top of it until he found the candle. It was a blocky red candle with a plastic wreath around its base. He couldn't remember where it had come from. He hadn't celebrated Christmas since he had lived with an aunt for two years many years ago. He remembered going to midnight mass with her, then eating some kind of pudding. He tried, as always, to remember how old he had been, but as always, it didn't come to him. He recalled the flavor of that pudding and it tasted like butterscotch, but he knew it wasn't. That aunt had died. Her name was Sandra, or Susan, or something that started with an S. Sometimes he liked to think that if she hadn't died, he would have lived with her forever. She liked midnight mass and she liked many men in those two years. But he remembered most that she liked him.

He lit the candle and picked up his sister's letter. In the yellow light he read, and it was full of the usual things—her job, her social life, the men who turned out to be drips or lechers, a guided tour of the places she had been to, and finally the offer to pay his way to Washington, D.C., and to get him a job. Loney had to smile because each of her letters for the past three or four years had contained this offer. It was an offer made in earnest, but Loney could not conceive of a life in the East. She would have better luck trying to convince a zebra to live in Washington. And so he read the three pages with a kind of guilty amusement until he reached the last paragraph, which was written in a hasty scrawl with a different-colored ink, green:

Since you do not choose to answer my letters and because I consider you my God-given burden in life, I have decided to take the week off at the end of this month and fly out. I would like to make it Thanksgiving, but I will be in Arizona at a meeting, *after which* I will fly to Great Falls, then to Havre. I will let you know when you can pick me up. Is your car running? Please be healthy. And *please* don't tell Dad I'm coming. It would only lead to difficulties unimaginable.

And it was signed, "Affectionately, Kate."

Loney lit a cigarette from the candle and found his hand trembling. It was not a new thing; lately it happened quite often, and he didn't know if it was a physical thing or if it was just because of the cigarettes and wine and lack of sleep. He made fists until the knuckles turned white, but still his hands shook. And again, as he had that night after the football game, he saw things strangely, yet clearly. The candle, the wine bottle, the letter before him, all burned clearly in his eyes and they had no reality in his mind. It was as though there were no connection between his eyes and his brain. And he saw the smoke ring go out away from his face and he saw the bird in flight. Like the trembling, the bird was not new. It came every night now. It was a large bird and dark. It was neither graceful nor clumsy, and yet it was both. Sometimes the powerful wings beat the air with the monotony of grace; at other times, it seemed that the strokes were out of tune, as though the bird had lost its one natural ability and was destined to eventually lose the air. But it stayed up and Loney watched it until it reached into the darkness beyond the small candlelight.

Loney picked up his glass. It was half full of wine. "Here's to the bird, my bird," he said. His mouth was dry and the wine did not taste good. He was restless. He had been thinking of his life for a month. He had tried to think of all the little things that added up to a man sitting at a table drinking wine. But he couldn't connect the different parts of his life, or the various people who had entered and left it. Sometimes he felt like a amnesiac searching for the one event, the one person or moment, that would bring everything back and he would see the order in his life. But without the amnesiac's clean slate, all the people and events were as hopelessly tangled as a bird's nest in his mind, and so for almost a month he had been sitting at his table, drinking wine, and saying to himself, "Okay, from this very moment I will start back—I will think of yesterday, last week, last year, until all my years are accounted for. Then I will look ahead and know where I'm going." But the days piled up faster than the years receded and he grew restless and despondent. But he would not concede that his life had added up to nothing more than the simple reality of a man sitting and drinking in a small house in the world.

And so he drank to the bird which came every night and he tried to attach some significance to it, but the bird remained as real and as elusive as the wine and cigarettes and his own life.

Swipesy whimpered in his sleep and Loney came back. He picked up the letter and turned again to the last paragraph. *The end of this month.* November. But he had no idea what the date was. He tried to think of something that had happened that would help, but the only thing he could think of was snow. And Rhea. He hadn't seen her for several days, since the trip out to Mission Canyon. He would see her soon. He would clean up again and he would see her. Like a first anniversary. They had met almost a year ago at a basketball game.

She had been selling tickets and she had been curt with him because she did not consider it part of her duties as an English teacher to sell tickets to a basketball game. But then she apologized and they talked for a few minutes. Loney had flattered himself that she recognized him from his picture in the trophy case at school. He had been on the team that won Harlem's only state championship. In the picture he was kneeling beside Myron Pretty Weasel, who was holding the basketball that read STATE B CHAMPS 1958. But she hadn't seen the picture; in fact, she hadn't even noticed the trophy case.

But a couple of weeks later she did recognize him in the grocery store. On an impulse she invited him home for dinner and she slept with him that night. They were both surprised. Loney couldn't believe that such a lovely classy woman would want him and Rhea couldn't believe it either. She had come north to escape entanglements. She told him this later. She admitted that at first he represented only warmth and sex. He had settled for that, but now, a year later, they were lovers and he was blowing it. And he didn't know why.

November. *This month.* He picked up the envelope and read the postmark: November 12. It must be the fifteenth or sixteenth. The candle flickered in a sudden draft of wind that rattled the back door. Kate would be here in two weeks. Loney poured himself a glass of wine.

The Death of Jim Loney: Indian or Not?

◆

Kathleen Sands

In many ways James Welch's second novel, *The Death of Jim Loney*, is clear-cut and straightforward, a narrative of alienation, progressive isolation, and death. Were it not a novel by an American Indian author, with a protagonist who is Gros Ventre half-breed, it might be adequate to characterize this as another in the growing numbers of alienation novels. Too simple. This is an unsettling yet strangely satisfying novel filled with ambiguity intensified by the complication of its none-too-apparent Indianness. But an Indian novel it definitely is, and examining the text as a work of Indian literature reveals why this dark ironic novel is ultimately consoling.

The usual way to prove a novel is Indian and to use the evidence as a critical tool is to point to an Indian author and analyze the ethnographic authenticity of customs and life ways in the work, point to influences of the oral tradition, concern with the landscape, and the collapse of sequential time. But with *Loney* such approaches are only partially successful. What little obvious ethnography appears is incidental—identification of tribe, a few tribal names, tribal cops, the reservation agency, vague references to ancient Indians fighting, gathering chokecherries in a particular spot, petroglyphs, but no ceremonies or traditional practices. Loney is too detached from his traditions to know, rediscover, or consciously utilize traditions. The landscape is no more useful. True, Loney is attached to the landscape. He can't leave it for "the good life" his sister Kate promises him in Washington, D.C., and even though he knows his lover Rhea's plan to go to Seattle could be a way out of his malaise, he can't take it, but not because he feels real affection for the land. He's indifferent to most of it and doesn't much like the butte that is the central focus of place in the novel, fears the sense of "lives" he feels out there—he just can't conceive of a life in the East, or in Seattle, or *life* anywhere. As in other Indian fiction, a sense of place is well developed, but for Loney the landscape isn't a potent force and not a healing one. He resists it, feels the "dim walls watching him" (Harper and Row edition, 89). The petroglyphs are dark, undecipherable omens that make him uneasy. The only way he can claim the landscape is in terms of death: "Once in a while I look around and see things familiar and I think I will die here. It's my country then" (107).

Is this alienation from the land a crisis of spirit similar to Tayo's in *Ceremony* or Abel's in *House Made of Dawn?* No. Loney has never had the traditional view of the land those protagonists can rediscover. Abandoned by his Gros Ventre mother when a year old and raised by his embittered non-Indian father for ten years, then abandoned again, this time to his father's mistress, Loney has no grounding in the stories or traditions that animate landscape. He feels the forces of the butte; his intuitions are sound, but he has no way to interpret the significance of either. Not until very near the end of the novel does he know anything of his mother, and he never learns any details of her past or of tribal traditions. She visits him in dreams—like the petroglyphs, she is an omen but undecipherable. Only when he finally confronts his father and forces recognition as his son does he get some answers to the questions about her that haunt his dreams, but even then the story is brief, only partly true, and he recognizes his father's lie. The oral tradition has ceased to flow and nurture. Unlike the protagonist in Welch's first novel, there can be no sudden understanding—isolation is finalized in Loney's father's lie; acknowledged as a son, he is orphaned again.

So what we might expect to contribute to some unraveling of the novel, landscape, oral traditions, Indian customs and life ways, in Welch's hands are ironic and defeating. When Loney reluctantly accompanies his old basketball teammate, Pretty Weasel, on a hunting expedition, there is at least mild anticipation that he may get in touch with traditions and the land and solve his isolation through symbolic quest—it worked for Tayo in *Ceremony* but he was prepared.

Loney's trip goes suddenly awry. No birds, no deer—a bear where there could be no bears. Then the fatal accident that Loney suspects is not accidental. He has shot, not the bear, but Pretty Weasel and sealed his own death in a moment that seems outside time or place. The hunt is reversed and Loney is now the hunted. He considers escape to Canada but rejects that. This is the country in which he will die. The situation, while unsought, is inevitable, a crisis effected by the accumulation of wrong moves and indecision.

Throughout the novel Loney fears life, fears pleasure, love, new experiences. Rhea and Kate both think of him as scaring off easily (44). For Loney, reality is not a comfortable place, the present not a comfortable time. He thinks of himself as ineffective and behaves inappropriately: in not confronting his father sooner, in not fulfilling his sister's expectations, in not returning Rhea's love better, in not eating, in drinking too much, in brooding and isolating himself. He knows he does not live even adequately. When Rhea envies him mildly for being able to choose between two sets of ancestors (14), he wishes he were one or the other, not both, as if that would solve his sense of disconnectedness. But the disconnection is not just from the past, it is from the present. His dog dies; his sister finally gives up on him; his lover resolves to leave for warmer territory; his father doesn't even feel guilty about rejecting him. In the disconnectedness, there is some sense of time collapse. The novel covers little more than a month, but it pulls the distant past strongly into the sequence of rather inconsequential events that leads up to the shooting in the cattails. There is a correspondent deterioration of reality and inclination toward waking dreams. It is the slow accumulation of events, both from the present and the past, that though apparently disconnected, as Welch presents them episodically and increasingy interentangled, effects Loney's removal from life. Present and past tangle but do not integrate. Time collapses but it does not merge in any sort of "Indian" way.

Are Loney's alienation and death a sort of dirge for the half-breed who can't determine his own identity and thus fails the world and himself? Hardly. Welch is too intelligent and subtle to opt for such simplistic schmaltz, the novel too serious to be a kind of dark joke. For Loney, life is a puzzle. If he could just understand his visions, his dreams, the petroglyphs, perhaps he could make sense of his life, begin to live it. For the reader it is a puzzle too. In a sense all the episodic incidents of the novel do merge—toward death. The novel opens with a biblical quotation: "Turn away from man in whose nostrils is breath, for of what account is he?" And in moments Loney does turn away from the football players with their breath steaming into the night air. Even before the beginning of the novel, however, Loney has turned away from life: in the narrative we see only a small, though intense, portion of his withdrawal. We see that relations with people are incidental, accidental, fleeting; we suspect they always have been. Even when he is with Kate or Rhea he is aware of the futility of his relationship, as though he were grieving over a loss in advance. It is not an unmotivated response; he has already lost his parents, his "aunt," his sense of a past. He seems a man in mourning for his own inability to engage, to live, a man mourning his own death. In his dream of his mother, she is searching for her son in a graveyard. She knows he is not there, not yet, but out in the mountains, but still she searches and grieves over his loss (33). The dream is Loney's imaginative projection, the mourning mother his invention. If there is truth in dreams, he is dead to himself. Is it any wonder he is so detached from life?

At one point Loney weeps for himself as though in mourning. In a kind of drunken stupor he "sees" the people most important to him viewing him from outside his window. He stands with them observing his own tears and explains to them that he weeps because he has no family, "no one." The explanation of the novel and projection of ensuing action, down to the shotgun his father eventually gives him, is contained in this vision, and in the recurring vision of the bird that alternates between graceful and awkward movement, as Loney does, perhaps representing his desire to be free of life's burdens and soar to a spirit world. From somewhere within his imagination, Loney uncovers the truth in his dreams and lives out his deepest insights. If such an "intuitive" interpretation sounds naive and like a rehash of cheap romanticism about Indians, it's not. The importance of dreams and visions and their form as presented in the novel draws support from tradition. For the Gros Ventre seeking for direction in life through vision was not a boyhood endeavor but an ordeal taken on in full manhood (Loney is in his mid-thirties). The seeker fasted, cried profusely, and saw spirits in waking visions as well as dreams, spirits that appeared as real people. Like Loney, the seeker "cried incessantly until he was exhausted and fell asleep."[1] If this is not an ethnographic detail one expects to find in an Indian novel, Welch undeniably has struck upon an imaginative moment that rings psychologically true. He appears uninterested in obvious aspects of ethnographic accuracy but specially sensitive to actions that relate to tribal character. Loney has no awareness of how Indian he is in his window hallucination or in his bird visions, but the reader, even without ethnographic information, senses that Loney's puzzling intuitions are essentially from his Indian nature, and Loney himself recognizes this when he feels that understanding them will somehow allow him to comprehend that part of his past connected to his mother.

Well before Loney kills Pretty Weasel and the pace of his doom accelerates, events in the novel tell us his death is a foregone conclusion and if this were simply a novel of alienation we might concede his death is meaningless, a predictable acting out of despair, a dark ending for a dark narrative. But the conclusion is not empty. It is in the conclusion that Loney finally takes control, makes decisions, behaves deliberately and effectively. He carefully chooses the time and place of his death despite his vulnerability and confusion. He ties up the loose ends of his life by confronting his father, spending a few loving hours with Rhea and resolving the dream of his mother by confirming to himself that his death will be a beginning free from the pain of the past. This deliberateness, of course, indicates that Loney's death is a form of suicide toward which he has been moving steadily throughout the novel, not the kind of mindless accident/suicide that Yellow Eyes, his mother's stepson, underwent, struck down by a train and barely mentioned in the papers, but an honorable act that faces the impossibility of achieving connectedness in life. As Loney leaves Rhea's apartment, he sets out like a Gros Ventre warrior, on foot and carrying the few supplies he will need[2]—a gun and whiskey to warm him. He has already announced his intention publicly by telling his father his destination, confident the old man will give the information to the authorities. Again, Gros Ventre custom is adhered to: "it was customary for a man who had something discreditable to account for to publicly announce that he was about to die."[3] As he progresses toward the butte to take his stand, he moves from fear and disorientation to a kind of trance-like state, partly caused by the cold and exertion and liquor. This, too, is in keeping with a state of mind recorded in Gros Ventre warriors: "even the bravest of men might **experience acute fear . . . their minds seemed not quite clear . . . the** effect was similar to drinking too much whiskey."[4] As the novel moves toward conclusion, the ambiguity and disconnectedness of the body of the narrative is resolved, each character and incomplete episode addressed and satisfied, so that when Loney reaches the butte he is truly isolated and everything converges on his death. But what does his death signify?

Loney's solitary stand is not ritually symbolic, a futile "statement" about Indian self-destructiveness. His death is simply what it appears to be, the best answer to an insoluble dilemma, an honorable act which will eradicate the past and fulfill his yearning to be relieved of life. He has already mourned his death sufficiently, and the loss of everyone of importance to him, and that grief motivates his final demand that death come to him. He does not seek it; he waits for it to arrive. In traditional times, "men who were grieving over the loss of loved ones were believed to have been especially prone to this indirect method of suicide," and "the most daring men in battle were said to have been those who wished to die."[5] Like an ancient warrior, Loney takes a position from which there is no retreat, and waits for the attack, even taunting the enemy and revealing his position. Any other action (flight, submission to prison) would be dishonorable and unacceptable. Though he can't live well "he couldn't think of a way *in the world* to be good enough" (37), he can die well. For months, actually for thirty-four years, life has been running out for Loney, so it is appropriate that he precipitates his own death, and that the novel ends as he watches his blood run down his arm and drip onto the earth.

Elements of ambiguity in the novel seem effectively resolved in the end, not glibly through use of formulaic patterns, but through a persuasive psychological reality that rings true to the Indian aspect of Loney's personality and circumstance, and is recognizably grounded in elements of tradition and supported by controlled and rather delicate infusions of qualities usually assoiciated with Indian literature. The relation of this novel to the canon of Indian fiction is perhaps less obvious than we have come to expect. It makes no confirmation of survival, provides no way to heal. It is a very terminal novel. If there is renewal, it is solely spiritual, the soaring of the spirit/bird, a final ambiguity in a complex work. *Loney* is undeniably a novel of alienation, but not a novel of emptiness or despair. Loney's death is not a futile act of annihilation but an appropriate and satisfying conclusion to a painful and solitary detachment from life. In this novel Welch has perhaps expanded American Indian fiction.

Notes

[1] Alfred Kroeber, *Ethnology of the Gros Ventre*, Anthropological Papers of the American Museum of Natural History (New York, 1908), pp. 221-222.

[2] Kroeber, p. 190.

[3] Regina Flannery, *The Gros Ventre of Montana*, Catholic University of America Anthropological Series, 15, Part 2 (Washington, D.C., 1953), p. 92.

[4] Flannery, p. 106.

[5] Flannery, p. 107.

The Dance of Jim Loney

◆

William Thackeray

Jim Loney is a halfbreed.

That's the principal fact of his life and the cause of his death. He dies of being a halfbreed, not an urban Indian or an off-reservation Indian, but a halfbreed.

Harlem, Montana, "just off the reservation," as James Welch tells us, is too straggly and insignificant to be urban. It is 60% watering hole for those Indians from Fort Belknap reservation who bypass the agency store "to go to town," 40% headquarters for a few down-at-the-heels White farmers and cowboys with their rusty pickups and their gleaming 30-06s in the back window. Jim Loney comes from half way between, where the cowboys met the Indians and used them and moved on. He's too stubborn and honest and aloof to be White or Indian. He's a halfbreed.

In Val Marie, where he played basketball, that endless reservation game of war, being a halfbreed means something. As the melodic French name reminds us, being a halfbreed in Canada means, at the very least, being a *Metis*, a mixed-blood, a descendant of the Northwest Resistance and of the heroes of the battles at Duck Lake and Batoche, where the rebellion was finally broken. "Batoche is the heart of the Metis People...," says a 1985 brochure, whose cover tells us, "The Metis People commemorate the Centenary of the Northwest Resistance: 1885-1985." Being a halfbreed in Canada gives one an identity and a heritage. The *Metis* are by law an "aboriginal culture."

Being a halfbreed in Harlem, Montana, means nothing—less than nothing, a negative cipher. In Harlem, Montana, being a halfbreed, being Jim Loney, gives you a choice of trying to live Indian or trying to live White. There is no such thing as living halfbreed. To live halfbreed is to be dead.

During the course of the novel, Jim Loney tries out both ways. His sister is a good role model. She lives White successfully, and his Indian mother, as everyone tells him, is crazy, so he tries White. His girlfriend is White, a teacher; she professes to love him, but what is it that she loves. Living with a White wife in a White man's house with a White man's dog and TV is not enough. The dog dies, frozen upright in the ice of the rutted street. To live White is to live a lie, unless one qualifies by being White.

Like all eternal questing orphans, Jim Loney seeks his father. A White father may give him an identity. But unlike the anonymous narrator of Welch's "Indian" novel, *Winter in the Blood*, Jim Loney's discovery of his ancestry, his father, is a revelation of despair not a revelation of distinguished heritage. To live White like his father is to be a cadging drunk in a beat-up, stinking trailer house across the tracks. To live White in Harlem, Montana, is no assurance of sanctity and a new life. To live White successfully, a halfbreed, like Loney's sister, must leave Harlem, Montana. But Loney won't leave, not until he has tried out that fundamental and most vivid dream of all us halfbreeds. The great adventure! Why not dance? Why not live Indian?

There's Pretty Weasel. Pretty Weasel wants to be his friend; he is always after him to go hunting. Pretty Weasel is a modern money-making Indian, but he still likes to hunt. On the reservation you can hunt without licenses and ordinances. You can still hunt like it meant something, like an Indian.

But a halfbreed cannot be Indian anymore than he can be White. The halfbreed's rhythm is too much White, too much the rhythm of death, the dance of death. The Great Bear Spirit—the power of the bear—is too bright for Jim Loney. He sees only the blinding light, and his White man's gun flares. Pretty Weasel is dead. Now, Jim Loney knows for certain he can't live Indian.

Unlike the narrator of *Winter in the Blood*, he does not have a sudden revelation—a vision—that shows him he is really Indian after all. Instead, Jim Loney's vision, the Indian way for him is a murderous farce. Even when they are hunting animals, White men think they hunt men. They kill their own kind. The animal spirits themselves rebel.

Jim Loney can't be Indian and he can't be White. But being halfbreed is being dead, without place, without heritage, without identity. Death becomes Jim Loney's mission.

He visits his father again and tells him the story, knowing his father will betray him. To make sure, he shoots up his father's trailer. And, of course, his father does betray him, as every Indian knows every White man will always betray him.

He visits his girlfriend one last time, but he is already dead. His mission of death takes him to Mission Canyon. He doesn't stay in the quiet womb of the canyon. He climbs the rock walls and crouches above the rock-face to wait. If he were Magua of old, he would try to escape up the rock-face and be picked off at the last second by Hawkeye, Deerslayer, Leatherstocking. But Magua's powerful resentment has become only a mission of indifference leading to one's own death.

When the hunters come, Jim Loney stands against the skyline, not unlike the heroic Cree, Almighty Voice, who stood off the Canadian army. His former basketball rival, who stands behind him in the picture of the basketball team in the high school annual, shoots him down. His killer is the Indian Leatherstocking. Like Leatherstocking, the turncoat White man who lives like an Indian, he is the turncoat Indian, who hunts men down like a White man to kill them.

So what does it all mean, the halfbreed's choice of death? Where does it fit the scheme of things? In Harlem, Montana, it means there is no life on the interstices. In dialectic, dichotomous America we get two choices: White, Indian; White, Black; rich, poor; success, failure; good, bad; alive, dead. There is no life half-way between. There is no half-way, no halfbreed, no dance, no adventure.

Jim Loney's is the tragedy of any man who is only half-way in a land that recognizes only make-it or not make-it, there or not there. You can choose to be either there or not there, but you can't choose to dance on the interstices between, where the halfbreed has his being.

Notes

[1]*James Welch.* Western Writers Series No. 57. Boise: Idaho State University, 1983.

[2]*Riding the Earthboy 40.* Rev. ed. New York: Harper & Row, 1976. p. 33.

[3]*Life Studies.* New York: Farrar Straus, 1956. pp. 89-90.

Transcendental Survival: The Way the Bird Works in *The Death of Jim Loney*

◆

Dexter Westrum

In James Welch's *The Death of Jim Loney* the protagonist Jim Loney, a mixed blood living a pointless existence in small town Montana, is troubled by recurring dreams of a bird which he sees as "a vision sent by (his Indian) mother's people."[1] Critics Kathleen Sands and Peter Wild disagree about the importance of this bird. Sands wonders if perhaps the bird represents Loney's desire to be free of life's burdens and soar "to a spirit world."[2] Wild feels the "bird is a heavy-handed and ill-defined symbol."[3] But neither critic explains exactly how the symbol works within the novel. My own contention is that the bird symbolizes the survival and fulfillment which comes about when the protagonist becomes aware of his own Indianness. The terms "survival" and "fulfillment," however, would seem not to bear upon the case of Jim Loney who never does understand his Indian ancestry and who physically dies as the novel concludes. But a look at the use of the mystical bird symbolism within the text will show that Loney's survival and fulfillment transcend the merely physical.

The metaphor for Jim Loney's life is established when the novel opens on Loney watching the final seconds of a football game. Harlem, the home town, is behind 13-6. Then they score. In an attempt to win the game, Harlem elects to fake kick on the conversion: "The holder scooped the ball off the ground and started to circle right .... The kicker followed him, dancing behind him like a thin bird"(2). The kicker runs into him and both fall in the mud while the ball hangs in the air above them. The ball lands on the thin player's back; he rolls over, pulls it to his belly, and lies there "without moving"(2). Like the holder, Loney is followed around by a bird—at least, by the dream of a bird. Since the bird seems to him to represent Indianness, we can see that the two players represent Loney's two distinct heritages. But the two bloodlines do not cause Loney to be any better coordinated than the two players on the field. The mixed bloodlines do not conflict so much as they simply do not mesh. At the same time the two players can be said to represent Loney and each of his three closest benefactors— his woman friend Rhea, his sister Kate, and his high school buddy Myron Pretty Weasel. All try to bring meaning to his life (as seemingly a completed pass would enhance the life of the thin player), but without plan or purpose Loney seems to render their efforts ineffectual. Just before Harlem scores, one of the fans says, "We're shit out of luck. What can you do in forty seconds?"(2). Actually, the team has all the luck and time in the world, but it simply doesn't execute the final play as if it knows what it's doing. Loney, too, has plenty of time and the good luck to have friends who care about him, but with one exception he does not seem able to execute the plays of his life.

Loney is a part-time agricultural laborer who doesn't mind when rain keeps him from work. Ambition does not seem to plague him: "his needs were few and not great in his mind" (3) and "he doesn't seem to care"(5). One thing, however, does bother him. When Rhea comments that Loney's mixed ancestry must be a fine thing, Loney doesn't answer her, but thinks: "It would be nice to think that one was one or the other, Indian or white. Whichever, it would be nicer than being a half-breed"(4). Loney is neither one nor the other; he is a man without a strong cultural identity.

This lack of cultural identity is exacerbated in that Loney does not have a strong personal identity. He did not grow up in a nurturing family. His mother "didn't exist. She left when (he) was a year old"(16) and his father Ike "left when (Loney) was nine or ten"(16) and was gone for twelve years. Even though Ike has returned to Harlem, he and Loney do not speak. Loney has been waiting for his father to approach him, but he guesses Ike doesn't "think (it) is worth it"(17). His sister Kate left him, too, before he was ten because she had a chance "to go to a better place"(90). They have seen each other only a few times since then. He is, as his name implies, alone.

Rhea romanticizes Loney, loving his "dark skin and (his) dark hair, (his) noble dark profile"(12). She knows Loney's life is empty and feels it is "up to her to give him . . . purpose"(27). She dreams of "starting fresh in a place where neither of them had been"(26). By the novel's end Rhea wants "mostly to be gone"(134) from Harlem. Her hope is that Loney will accompany her to Seattle and start fresh.

Loney knows Rhea loves him, but he also knows he is "blowing"(22) the relationship. He loves "being with her (but can't) admit to himself that he (does) need her"(37). The decision to leave for Seattle is too hard for him to make; he wants only to "sit on his step and think"(48). He will not commit a decisive act. He tells her: "I don't want you to go, but I don't have enough in me to make you want to stay"(107). Loney cannot bring himself to accept the possibilities that a new life might bring. He doesn't decide against Rhea so much as he simply fails to decide at all.

Loney's sister Kate is a federal bureaucrat who sees him as her "God-given burden in life"(19). She loves her brother "more than anything"(63) and it breaks "her heart to think of him"(63). She knows education has "gotten her up and out of a dismal existence (and expects) it could do the same for others"(165). She is bothered that Loney doesn't seem to realize that he's "as smart as anybody"(75). She wants him to live with her in Washington, D.C., where he'll have "things that would arouse (his) curiosity, give (him) some purpose"(76). Kate's concern for Loney is like "that of a lover seeking a perfect love"(89), and when she can't persuade him to leave she feels as "crushed as a rejected lover might"(89). She tells him: "You are not a part of (my life) anymore, by your own choosing. You have nothing left. Anything you do from now on you will do without conviction, without spirit"(88). Loney knows Kate is "suffering . . . because of him"(133), but he cannot bring himself to act as she wants.

Myron Pretty Weasel considers Loney to be "the last friend he'd had"(82). They played together on the high school basketball team. He wonders how Loney, the "smart one"(82) in high school could have fallen into this "desperado life"(82). Pretty Weasel tries to rekindle their adolescent friendship. He throws "his arm around Loney's shoulder"(96), hits him on the arm, and makes "a grab for Loney's nuts"(114) in the playful manner of high school athletes. Even though Myron never has been a smoker, he has a cigarette with Loney "as a kind of offering"(101). To further rebuild their friendship, Pretty Weasel suggests they go hunting and even provides Loney with a rifle,

a 30-30. Unfortunately, Pretty Weasel becomes the victim of his own
efforts to invest Loney's life with meaning. Loney apparently mistakes
him for a bear in a stand of cattails and kills him. The hunting trip,
however, leads Loney to his only truly decisive act of the novel. He
decides to take charge of his own destiny. He remembers that they had
seen a bear before he shot Myron even though there "were no bears
anymore (because they) had been driven out of the valley years
ago"(117). He begins to think "of the bear not as a bear but as an agent
of evil"(129). The killing becomes a complex act for Loney:

> That it was accident did not occur to Loney. That the
> bear, as rare and inexplicable as its appearance had
> been, was simply a bear did not occur to him either.
> And so he was inclined to think that what had
> happened happened because of some quirky and pre-
> dictable fate . . . Because his consciousness had
> dimmed in the past couple of months... he didn't know
> that he had in that moment devised an end of his own
> (129-130).

Equipped with this sense of a predictable fate, Loney carries out "a
dim plan that he (doesn't) understand"(149). He feels "part of something
bigger than his life"(149). He tells his father whom he visits for a talk
after long silence that he "think(s he) killed (Myron) on purpose"(148).
Ike encourages him to run, but Loney tells him he is going to Mission
Canyon on the reservation because "that's the best place"(149). His
father gives him money and a sixteen-gauge shotgun. As he leaves his
father's trailer, Loney, whose head is "very clear"(150), turns and
shoots out the lights because he knows his father will "squeal"(163)
—tell the police about the killing. For the first time in the novel, Loney
is "in control"(174). When the police track him to Mission Canyon, he
shoots at their car: "He couldn't hope to reach the car from his position,
but he didn't mean to"(177). Loney intends only to call attention to
himself with the shot: "Loney want(s) to be found"(178). In response to
the harmless blast, the grim Indian policeman Doore sights Loney in
the scope of a high-powered rifle and kills him. As Loney falls, he
thinks, "This is what you wanted"(179).

Loney's first and last major purposeful act in the novel is to
engineer his own death. The accident has brought Loney out of his
meaningless life:

> He becomes a man of action . . . He realizes he
> has done something traumatic here and he takes the
> blame for it . . . . He treats himself as a criminal.
> And he plants clues around so the cop will know to
> find him in Mission Canyon and he knows which cop
> will come to get him and he knows that cop won't be
> afraid to shoot him. To create one's own death is a
> positive way of acting.[4]

What makes the act positive is that in electing death Loney is transcending life as he knows it. He is beginning to sense a reality beyond three dimensions. This contention is supported within the text by Loney's relationship with his dog Swipesy, his memory of a Bible verse from Isaiah, and the recurring vision of the bird which seems to be a symbol of Indianness.

Loney's dog is "very old and deaf"(12) and never barks any more (46). Loney sees the dog as an example: "I think you understand everything about life...You live clean and you never abuse yourself... I just wish I was as smart as you"(18). In Loney's mind Swipesy is smart enough to know that he is a tired old dog "ready to die"(53). When the dog turns up missing, Loney searches for him but he knows the animal will "not be back"(49). Eventually he finds the dog frozen in the mud. Seven-year-old Amos After Buffalo is staring at the dead dog. With the help of the boy's knife, Loney cuts Swipesy out of the mud. Amos advises Loney to "bury him out there (and points) in the general direction of the Little Rockies"(54). As Loney walks away cradling the dog, Amos thinks it's "funny that the man didn't seem to be sad about his dog"(55). Loney isn't sad because he doesn't think "of him as being dead"(108). In fact, when Loney is enroute to Mission Canyon, which is in the Little Rockies, he walks through Amos's village and he tells an indifferent village dog to tell Amos "you saw me carrying a dog and that I was taking that dog to a higher ground"(167). At the same time Loney would like to spare Amos the bleak future that he sees for him: "Amos, if I could, I would take you with me, right now, and spare you sorrow. I might survive. Oh, God, we might survive together"(167). Loney's use of "survive" here when he knows that he is arranging his own death supports the idea that such a death will not be the end of life. Death will simply be the means by which he attains "a higher ground."

This idea is supported by Isaiah 2:22 which Loney has been

remembering for no apparent reason: "Turn away from man in whose nostrils is breath, for of what account is he"(1). In Isaiah the people of Israel are instructed to turn away from the ways of man and go up the mountain of the Lord to learn his ways and walk in his paths. Loney, then, is actually on a mission as he heads into Mission Canyon. He is turning away from his life. He sees himself "in control"(174), "out here in these mountains waiting"(175). He know there has to be "a place where . . . everything was all right and it was like everything was beginning again . . . but it (is) not on this earth"(175). The Bible verse supports Loney's notion here, but Loney is not consciously Christian. At the same time, he is not consciously Indian. The meaning of the bird vision frustrates him as much as the meaning of the Bible verse. In fact, the symbolic value of the bird appears never to be actually known to Loney. The text offers us the bird—and the verse, as well—as a way of explaining what is happening to Jim Loney. It explains the transcendent reality he is after, and it illustrates the manner in which Loney survives. We learn that the bird

> was a large bird and dark. It was neither graceful nor clumsy, and yet it was both. Sometimes the powerful wings beat the air with the monotony of grace; at other times, it seemed that the strokes were out of tune, as though the bird had lost its one natural ability and was destined to eventually lose the air. But it stayed up (20).

Like Loney, the bird is not a set and constant entity. He moves gracefully with Rhea, yet he is clumsy with his emotions. He is out of tune with himself; he has no idea who he really is. He is neither Indian nor white, yet he is both. And being both he doesn't have the natural ability to be either. Like the bird, Loney's actual identity remains "real and elusive"(21). The visionary bird, even though it looks as if it will fall, manages to remain in flight. It does not crash. This aspect of continued flight becomes important when Loney physically dies.

In one of Loney's dreams, his father comments that Loney is as "(a)lone as that bird he would believe in"(24). This concept of Loney's aloneness is re-enforced during a romantic evening with Rhea when Loney sees his visionary bird in the fire. He wants "to share this moment"(30) with Rhea, but he knows she is not open to this world of visions from his mother's people. Worth noting here is that during the evening with Rhea, he watches "the bird getting smaller"(30) as if it were flying away. Later when Loney forces his father to speak to him he feels as if the silent past "had been nothing more than a bird disappearing in the night"(140). The bird appears to be diminished in the presence of whites. At the same time Ike is responsible for the fulfillment of the bird vision. When he forces the shotgun on his son, Loney remarks, "It's the perfect bird gun"(149). Without the gun Loney could not signal Doore who so effortlessly kills him.

As he stands eyes closed before the entrance to Mission Canyon, Loney's "mind is full of flickering images"(168), the scenes of his life. The scenes come "like dark birds"(168) until the bird-like scenes, Loney thinks "they brought me here"(168). He is right on more than one level. The scenes or events of his life have brought him to this place while at the same time the visionary birds have brought him on this mission. And the scene-birds are gone when he opens his eyes because when he enters Mission Canyon he leaves his life behind. But the bird from his mother's people is not part of the life he leaves behind. Indeed, as he falls after the fatal shot, he feels "a harsh wind where there (is) none (and sees) the beating wings of a dark bird as it climb(s) to a distant place"(179). The wind indicates his movement into a trans- cendent reality, to a distant place where everything is all right. He has symbolically achieved fulfillment through his Indianness in that he dies—indeed, has a mission to die—on Indian land. The only way to survive is not to survive within the confusion of his pointless existence. His transcendence is his triumph.

Welch is not saying here that the only way for mixed bloods to survive is to engineer their own physical deaths. He is saying that the way to fulfillment lies is discovering one's Indian identity. Since Jim Loney is not fortunate enough to have an actual link to his past, he is forced to rely on his instincts, and his transcendent fulfillment, however thin it may seem to those leading useful lives, carries him beyond the pointlessness of his existence.

Notes

[1]James Welch, *The Death of Jim Loney* (New York: Perennial Library, 1981; orig. pub. 1979), p. 105.

[2]Kathleen M. Sands, *"The Death of Jim Loney:* Indian or Not?" *Studies in American Indian Literature,* 5 (Fall 1981), p. 7.

[3]Peter Wild, *James Welch* (Boise: Boise State University, 1983), p. 43.

[4]James Welch, "American Indian Literature Today," panel discussion with James Welch, Gerald Vizenor, and Dexter Westrum, University of Minnesota, May 16, 1984. Critics who automatically rule out an author's words about his own work can take comfort in that Welch concluded the quoted remarks with the admission that "This could all be rationalization."

Women's Roles in Contemporary Native American Writing and in Welch's *The Death of Jim Loney*

◆

Ronald McFarland

Like most non-Indian children, my first notions of the Native American female were an amalgam of courageous Pocohontas throwing her young body over that of Captain John Smith to save him from execution; loyal Sacajawea guiding Lewis and Clark through uncharted Northwest wilds amidst hordes of hostile kinsmen; wise old Nokomis raising her grandson, Hiawatha, to manhood by the shores of Gitche Gumee.[1] (Hiawatha's wife, Minnehaha, somehow failed to impress me when I was a boy.) Courage, loyalty, and wisdom, however, are hardly the nouns that would come to mind if one were to define the Native American female as she exists in contemporary fiction. To a considerable degree, in fact, the Indian novel has remained the province of the alienated, culturally emascualted male, and the reasons for this may be fairly obvious. The traditional Indian male, warrior and hunter, has borne the heavier burden of the cultural holocaust. Moreover, one might argue that the female, whose cultural roles were less fully disrupted, finds it easier to adapt. I hope these conjectures are taken for the hypotheses that I intend them to be.It seems to me that in all the brooding and lamentation over what has become of the Native American male, the tragedy of the female has been to some degree overlooked, or at least overshadowed. Their dilemma has certainly not been ignored altogether, but the female characters have emerged among contemporary Indian writers as sort of shadow figures.

The traditional roles of Blackfeet women, as of other Native American women, are a matter reasonable accessible record.[2] In addition to preparing meals, the Plains Indian women participated in the slaughtering and extensive preparations of the buffalo, from buffalo robes made of its hide to glue made from its scrotum.[3] They were the fire tenders and the root and berry gatherers. In rearing their children, Indian mothers were important as conservators and transmitters of culture. James Willard Schultz, who lived among the Blackfeet between 1877 and 1903 and who wrote about them until his death in 1947, sums it up in an "old, old" tribal saying: "Men for the war trail, women for the home lodge."[4] The story Schultz tells thereafter, "A Bride for Morning Star," recounts the attempt of a Piegan named Lance Woman to follow the lead of a warrior woman named Running Eagle. At the end of the story, after she narrowly escapes being offered as a human sacrifice by the Pawnee, Lance Woman says: "I don't want to be a warrior-woman. I want to be a real woman. I want to have what all real women have, a lodge of my own."[5] Schultz also refers to the legend of Running Eagle, the warrior woman, in his story, "Cut-Nose," in which Otter Woman's father urges her to marry for a painfully practical reason: "Daughter, it is that every woman of our tribe should marry, should have children. All too few are our men. They fall in battle with our many enemies."[6] The best way for her to have vengeance on the Crows, he argues, is for her to raise strong, brave sons to fight them.

But if the Indian male has lost his identity as a warrior and hunter, so has the Indian female lost her identity as a wife and mother; and the wars, from World War II through Vietnam, which have offered temporary return of the male to his status as warrior, have brought no corresponding relief to the Indian woman. The Native American female, in fact, has had to deal both with the dislocations of the men and with the bitter aftermath of their return to a society which habitually disregards or even discards its warriors after the smoke of battle has cleared. The American Legion and Veterans of Foreign Wars posts do not adequately replace the council fire, but contemporary Indian writers have recounted, perhaps too often, how bars and taverns take up the slack. And as women once followed their men to the hunt or on the warpath, they now tend to follow them to the bars.

The most frequently recurring "type" of female character in contemporary Native American writing is the "bar woman." James

Welch offers two examples in *Winter in the Blood:* Agnes the Cree woman, who is the narrator's runaway girlfriend, and Malvina, who represents, according to A. Lavonne Ruoff, a "female castrator" and "what Agnes will probably be like at forty."[7] Leslie Silko's barwomen in *Ceremony* are Tayo's mother and the aimless Ute, Helen Jean, who leaves Tayo and his Laguna pals for a Mexican with a fresh paycheck, vowing not to "waste any more time fooling around with Indian war heroes."[8] Marnie Walsh, in her powerful four-poem sequence entitled "Vickie Loans-Arrow," offers a virtual family of bar women, from Aunt Nettie and Cousin Charlene to the title character herself.[9]

In *The Death Of Jim Loney* Welch's protagonist encounters a bar woman, and he does something unusual: he speculates on her type.

> He had been sitting by the woman for over two hours and it had been the same rough talk and he wondered what made some women so hard, especially bar women. When they reached a certain age they just got hard. Loney thought of the women he had seen who could sit on a stool all night without getting drunk, or at least visibly drunk, but when you looked into their eyes you sould see the hardness, as cold and hard as the January earth. He wondered what they were like at home, if they sent kids off to school in the morning, if they made cakes, if they made love, if they loved anyone. (p.36)

What is "unusual" about Loney's ruminations on the bar woman is that he does reflect upon the type; he *thinks* about them. Silko's protagonist, Tayo is the half-breed product of a bar woman, but his memories remain a series of ugly vignettes by which he haunted but about which he never really speculates. Of the two protagonists, Loney, whose mother also became a bar woman but whom he cannot remember, is clearly the more "intellectual" in the sense that he more often inclined to "think things out" than is Tayo. This does not, of course, mean that he is somehow superior to Tayo, but in so far as the two mixed-blood characters bear comparison, it is obvious that Tayo is much closer to what might be called his "Indian nature" than is Jim Loney. That fact more than any other may account for Tayo's ability to survive his cultural conflict. Both characters triumphantly assert their "Indianness," but Loney is killed in the process.

Against the "bar woman" type, most Native American writers portray, usually as what I would call "shadow figures," various types of the traditional Indian woman as nurturing wife/mother or as wise old grandmother. The grandmother, of course, is a link to the "old ways." She appears as Priest of the Sun Tosamah's Kiowa grandmother in N. Scott Momaday's *House Made of Dawn*[1] and as Tayo's "old Grandma" in Silko's *Ceremony*, where she provides a vital connection between the protagonist and Ku'oosh, the medicine man (the trail eventually leads to old Betonie). In Welch's *Winter in the Blood* the grandmother, whose age has been calculated to be over one hundred, never says a word, yet her presence is a constant reminder of the glorious and tragic Blackfeet past, and it is in his understanding of her mystery that the narrator dissolves the distance that has created the winter in his blood.

It is arguably the lack of this important liason with his Indian heritage that causes Jim Loney's struggle with his identity to be so painful. Old Emil Cross Guns, in fact, is the only link to the Indian past that Loney can recall, but he is dead, and as Loney reflects, "Everything was changed and the old ones did not exist" (p. 102). Loney admires his sister's "ability to live in the present," but he wonders at her "lack of need to understand the past" (p.88). Although she works for an Indian agency in Washington, D.C., his sister is in most ways less "Indian" than he. Loney's interest in the past is limited generally to his own futile efforts at recapturing his own childhood memories. If respect or reverence for the past indicates Indianness, then it is no wonder that Loney, who hopes for "some sort of controlled oblivion" (p. 59), can reflect that, "He never felt Indian" (p.102). It is one of the happy ironies of this often unhappy novel, therefore, that Jim Loney dies an Indian.

The other shadow figure, that of the nurturing wife and mother, has undergone an important transformation in Contemporary Native American writing. Whereas the father tends to be the missing person in the Black ghetto, the mother seems to be the most commonly absent figure on the reservation. Of course in many cases both natural parents are absent. Abel, in *House Made of Dawn*, is an orphan raised by his grandfather. The narrator of *Winter in the Blood* is raised by his mother, Teresa, but she remains a somewhat distant character, her inclination toward the White priest from Harlem being at odds with her marriage to Lame Bull.[12] Her son apparently approves of neither relationship. Silko in *Ceremony* and Welch in *The Death of Jim Loney* describe circumstances under which the protagonists are raised by surrogate mothers, an aunt in both instances.

Jim Loney tells Rhea that his mother "didn't exist" (p. 16), but in fact he actively searches for traces of both his natural and his surrogate mothers, a Catholic whose name was "Sandra, or Susan, or something that started with S" (p.19). At one point he has a long dream of a beautiful woman who describes herself as "A mother who is no longer a mother" (p. 34). Of his aunt, Loney's clearest memory is of ersatz butterscotch pudding: "The only thing he was sure of was that of all the women in his life, she was the one he had tried hardest to love" (p. 51). After he kills his old friend, Myron Pretty Weasel, whose mother also left home, Loney tries to find Sandra's grave, but in the process he concludes that he did not really love her after all (p. 133).

Loney then confronts his father for the full story of his natural mother, Electra Calf Looking, who appears to be either in prison in Nebraska or in the state hospital at Warm Springs from "a combination of booze and an excess of men"(p.70). Loney's father lies to him, saying that she is a nurse somewhere in New Mexico, but he sees through it, for in actuality he knows she was a bar woman and, too, his father has more than once called her a "whore." Near the end of the novel Loney recalls his dream of the young woman searching for her lost son, and he concludes that she (obviously his mother) "was not crazy....She was a mother who was no longer a mother. She had given up her son to be free and and that freedom haunted her...and so she had come back to him in his dream and told him that her son would not allow himself to be found...he was out in these mountains, waiting" (p. 175). Loney also concludes that there is a "place where people bought each other drinks and talked quietly about their pasts...where those pasts merged into one and everything was all right....No lost sons, no mothers searching." He locates that place, soon after, in his death.

Welch's *The Death of Jim Loney* may be singular in its presentation of an Indian woman who takes on the White world and deals with it successfully, at least in its own terms. This is Kate Loney, the protagonist's sister, who lives and works in Washington, D.C. We get our first impressions of her throught her letter to her brother's White girlfriend, Rhea, a letter described as "crisp" and "businesslike" (p. 25). The two most important living women in Loney's life share a

desire to "save" him by removing him from Harlem, Montana. Rhea
would lure him west, to Seattle, while Kate would draw him east, to
Washinton. Neither woman appears to perceive, as the confused
protagonist does, that his problems are internal and are best confronted
at home.

Kate is described as "six feet tall, lean and striking as a dark cat"
(p. 62). She is deliberately "Indian" in her dress. In purchasing her
squash blossom necklace directly from a Navaho silversmith, we are
told, Kate feels "righteous" (p.63). If the reader is intended simply to
believe that Kate loves but fails to understand her brother, which we
might infer from Anatole Broyard, one of Welch's harshest critics,[13]
then she is not a very consequential character in her own right. I
suggest, however, that Kate is a complex character who bears some
scrutiny on the reader's part. Welch sends a number of signals to this
effect, one of which is Kate's smugness: "She was here and she knew
what to do" (p.64). She leads her inebriated brother to a seat in the
terminal and places her leather briefcase on his lap. Always the
businesswoman, Kate has no intentions of letting her work slide while
she ministers to her ailing, wayward brother. She doesn't even ask
whether he has brought a car (he has), but proceeds to the car rental
counter where she allows her American Express card to do the
talking. While her brother has been cooped up in his car with a bottle,
she has been relaxing on a queen-sized bed at a Ramada Inn, her flight
delayed by a snowstorm. After he reiterates a third time that he
"thought about going home" but instead "waited for you," Kate
"realized that he was absolutely smashed, but she didn't even mind
that much" (pp. 63-64). This, the reader is inclined to say, is real big of
her.

We should also be suspicious of Kate when we detect her
condescending attitude toward "this small world" of northern
Montana, which she believes is "so simple and logical" (p.64). In fact,
Kate appears to have returned to her brother as much for a short
vacation as she has to try to save him from himself. She "knew they
couldn't" have the peaceful smalltown life she observes, and she is
convinced that he will return to his drinking as soon as she leaves.
Moreover, it is Kate who says to Rhea: "He is something of a toy" (p.85).
One might question whether Kate's mission of mercy is occasioned
more by love of her brother or jealousy over his relationship with
Rhea. She reveals, though not to Loney, that she separated from him

when they were children because she did not wish to "compete" with Sandra. Kate has, it would appear, very little capacity for love, and I think it is no oversight on Welch's part that after Loney says "I love you," and then feels "oddly cheerful" (p. 91), Kate says nothing. Jim Loney's friends, we are told later, used to call her "Ice Woman" when Kate was a teenager (p.111). What we learn about Kate during her first morning with her brother, though, is sufficient: "If they just sat at the table and talked all day, that would be good enough with her. But she did have to call her office sometime" (p. 65). The issue here, by the way, is not whether it is possible for a woman to have a profession and still be loving and responsive to the man or men in her life. It is simply that Kate has not managed to do so.

The record of contemporary Native American writers so far suggests that the image of the Indian woman has been at least as debased as that of the Indian male. Momaday, Silko, and Welch all show signs of hope for Indian males, but none of their female characters, with the exception of Silko's mystical Elk Woman (Ts'eh), who can hardly be regarded as an ordinary mortal, offer much grounds for optimism. The mother appears to be unable or unwilling to nurture her children. The grandmothers possess a wisdom that can redeem, but as Jim Loney realizes, they are dying out. The new generation of girl-friends, lovers, and mothers-to-be are represented on the one hand by the bar women (like Welch's Agnes and Walsh's Vickie Loans-Arrow) and on the other hand by the cold businesswoman, Kate Loney, who is, after all, every bit as alienated and lonely, despite her "success," as her brother.

The role of the Native American female has not been completetly accounted for, however, if that of the White woman is ignored. Writing about the development of literary myths on the American frontier, Richard Slotkin has noted that by the early nineteenth century, writers had discovered that "the Indian woman answers the longing of the American male soul for its missing, better half."[14] I suspect someting of a parallel sort may be said of the Indian male relative to the American female soul. Elsewhere in his study Slotkin argues that the "ethic of the white woman" is one of self-restraint and self-abnegation, whereas that of the Indian embodies, "the traits of the libido: sexual and conceptual energy, filled at once with creative and destructive potentialities."[15] Certainly the two prominent female characters in Momaday's *House Made of Dawn*, the doctor's wife from

California, Angela Grace St. John (as symbolically packed a name as one may find in all of literature), and Milly, the social worker, are White women in need of some spiritual or passionate expression of their "selves." Josiah's Mexican woman, Lalo, for Silko's *Ceremony*, may have something in common with such women, but the old cantina dancer generally seems to possess more of the mystique that Slotkin ascribes to Indians. The White women Silko depicts are more commonly those who fell prey to the Indian men when they were in uniform. They are recalled by Tayo's companions with disgust and bitterness, on the one hand as conquests, but on the other hand as reminders of the fact that their acceptance by White society was only temporary.

In Rhea Davis, Jim Loney's Dallas socialite-turned-schoolteacher lover, Welch portrays a woman who is virtually sinister in her superficiality. It is easy, on the one hand, to take her at face value, as she seems to take herself, and to regard her as a kind, loving woman trying desperately to "save" her mysteriously unreachable boyfriend. It is also easy to dismiss her, as does Anatole Broyard, as a superficial and confused coquette trying to administer a crash course in "life appreciation." In reality, however, Welch has created in Rhea a dangerous and destructive woman whose education and sophistication produce a veneer that causes the reader to forget how calculating she is, just as he or she may forget how "businesslike" Kate Loney is. The fact is that neither Rhea nor Kate offers Jim Loney the comforts of hearth and home (or lodge) or the reassurance of his masculinity which one might conventionally associate with the female, whether Indian or not.

In our first glimpses of her, we connect Rhea with "malaise," a sort of spiritual discontentment with a stylish, Romantic ring to it. She appears to be languishing, rather in the mode of a *fin-de-siecle* English society lady who is quite self-consciously bored. Her tea and English muffins combine with the image she paints of her parents (her father shooting clay pigeons and her mother doing watercolors) to reinforce our sense of her as a dillettante. But as Welch makes quite clear, she is more than a silly Southern belle "roughing it" in Big Sky country. She is an aggressive, devouring woman: "At least I have passion in me. And big white teeth. I could bite through a tree. 'Grrr,' she said" (p.8). Since this passage is humorous, we may tend to read through it without a second thought. But this is one of several references to

Rhea's teeth in the novel, and to slight its importance would be, I think, to miss Welch's message, that Rhea Davis is a ravenously hungry woman.

Throughout the novel, Rhea takes the initiative. Early on, she goes to Jim Loney's house to seduce him, and the language of their encounter is significant:

> "You're so damned lovely sometimes. Sometimes I
> think I would just like to take a bite of you."
> "We could go inside," said Loney.
> "I love your dark skin and your dark hair, your
> noble dark profile. Sometimes you remind me of a
> greyhound. Do you mind?"
> "You want to gnaw on my arm?"
> "I want to gnaw on your throat," she growled. (p. 12)

Much later in the novel, in their last love-making before Loney is killed, she bites his neck, then croons: "Oh Jim, you've been wonderful ....We've been wonderful" (p. 153). Loney may believe she loves him, but he stares at the ceiling rather than confirm this description of their relationship.

Rhea's character combines Romantic fancy with hard-nosed, realistic awareness of how to use people, especially men. Recalling the exhibit of cowboy art in the Amon Carter Museum, Rhea thinks of her delight at having projected herself into "another world," that of the Wild West. But she is dissatisfied with the real West, and she is disappointed, with Montana, which has turned out not to be all "summer theatres and mountains and Glacier Park" (p. 11). Perhaps the height of her insipidity occurs early in the novel, when she tells Loney how lucky he is since he" can be Indian one day and white the next. Whichever suits you" (p.14). Her Romantic projections, whether they concern place or character, remind one of Emma Bovary's, but Rhea is a modern woman and an American. Accordingly, she has much greater control over the situation, and even if we find her insensitive or superficial at times, we should remember that she is self-controlled, willful, and capable of being quite devious. Certainly her reflections on the affair with the SMU professor, a sort of game which "ended badly and bitterly" (p. 126), suggest that she used her "willed innocence" to advantage on that occasion. Moreover, she enjoys her power over men:

she "was used to men doing foolish things for her; sometimes she made them do foolish things"(p.31).

At age twenty-nine, with an M.A. in English from Southern Methodist University, Rhea must confess to Kate that before this job, which she has held just two years and which she is now leaving on short notice in the middle of the term, she "had never really worked at anything" (p.86). Not surprisingly, she also confesses Loney was at first a mere "diversion," a "toy," a "chance to be frivolous." She now insists that she loves him, but the reader must decide whether to believe her. But can a person so self-centered have much love to give? She and Loney rarely go to her house, and when they do, he senses a formality about her that probably indicates more than just "Southern hospitality." Rhea is a person who depends a great deal on form. After making love with Loney, she catches herself very carefully placing her crystal cigarette lighter exactly where she found it; then, as she watches him sleep, she lights a cigarette and wonders how she looks "drink in one hand, cigarette in the other"(p. 32). Perhaps the most obvious example of Rhea's egocentricity and of her tendency always to seize control is her anouncement to Loney of her plans to leave for Seattle (pp. 43-44). Put simply it amounts to the following: I'm bored here, whether you are or not, so I'm going to Seattle; I've heard it's beautiful (I know you've been there, but I haven't asked you about it); don't you think you'd like to come with me? She does not offer Seattle as an alternative choice, nor does she discuss with Loney her "dilemma"; she simply presents him with her decision and announces, in effect, that he may take it or leave it.

In his analysis of Chateaubriand's *Les Natchez* ("Atala" and "Rene," both written in the 1790's), Richard Slotkin observes that Chactas and Rene are "mixed characters, blending traits of both white and Indian—Christian reason and restraint, and Indian passion."[16] This obvious over-simplification probably has greater validity for early writing by White authors than it does for contemporary Native American writing. The latter events of *The Death of Jim Loney*, however, do cry out for some sort of "interpretation," for some clarifying set of generalizations. Except for her education at a church related university, there is little about Rhea Davis that is notably "Christian," but in some ways both she and Kate represent "reason and restraint," which in various instances can amount to avoidance of confrontation. Certainly we see both women as aloof and rational, even though they are under some pressure.

Jim Loney accepts neither of the options offered Rhea and Kate, and in truth they amount to little more than two versions of the same thing: denial of serious, deep confrontation of the self. But in killing his boyhood friend, Pretty Weasel, Loney appears to be rejecting the Indian way as well. Whether the shooting is accidental or not, however, matters less than how Loney acts afterwards. If he runs away or tries to alibi or deny responsibility for the shooting, he is doing little more than what Rhea and Kate have been urging all along. In returning to his traditional Indian male role as hunter and warrior, however, Jim Loney does confront his self and resolve his dilemma by facing up to it and by accepting the consequences of his action. And he does act. He does not end up as the passive, inert, dream-haunted nonperson he was earlier in the novel, nor does he simply evade his problems by running from them. It is important that the reader recognize Loney is not offered the option of hearth or lodge by nurturing, loving wife, sister, or mother. His choice is that of his Indian male ancestors: either retreat to unfamiliar ground, or fight to the death on native soil. The "sensible" choice from the White perspective would be to withdraw in some way or other (the maneuver was called "strategic withdrawal" a few years ago). Loney considers the problem very carefully, weighs his options, thinks, then decides not to do the sensible thing.

Notes

[1] For an example of how much myth may vary from reality on such matters, see David Remley's "Sacajawea of Myth and History" in *Women in Western American Literature*, Helen Winter Stauffer and Susan J. Rosowski, eds. (Troy, N.Y.: Winston, 1982), pp. 70-89. See also Leslie A. Fiedler's *The Return of the Vanishing American* (New York: Stein and Day, 1968), pp. 63-83.

[2] See John C. Ewer's *The Blackfeet: Raiders of the Northwest Plains* (Norman: University of Oklahoma, 1958) and Clark Wissler's *The Social Life of the Blackfoot Indians*, Anthropological Papers of the American Museum of Natural History, Vol. 7, Part 1 (New York, 1900).

[3] Ewers, pp. 73-6.

[4] James Willard Schultz, *Blackfeet and Buffalo* (Norman: University of Oklahoma, 1962), p. 347.

[5] Schultz, p. 367.

[6]Schultz, p. 230.

[7]A. Lavonne Ruoff, "Alienation and the Female Principle in *Winter in the Blood*," *American Indian Quarterly*, 4 (May 1978), p. 115. The essay is reprinted in this volume.

[8]Leslie Silko, *Ceremony* (New York: Viking, 1977), p. 166.

[9]Marnie Walsh, *A Taste of the Knife* (Boise: Ahsanta, 1976), pp. 1-11.

[10]James Welch, *The Death of Jim Loney* (New York: Harper and Row, 1979), p. 36. Other references to this Perennial Library paperback edition of the novel are included in the text.

[11]N. Scott Momaday, *House Made of Dawn* (New York: New American Library, 1969), pp. 83-91, 117-125.

[12]Ruoff, p. 113. She describes, too, the narrator's "Oedipal jealousy" and deprivation of affection.

[13]Anatole Broyard, Review, *New York Times* (November 28, 1979), C-25.

[14]Richard Slotkin, *Regeneration Through Violence* (Middletown, Connecticut: Wesleyan University, 1973), p. 326.

[15]Slotkin, p. 553. He is speaking of the Indian male here.

[16]Slotkin, p. 377.

Untitled
Novel
in
Progress

Selections from Untitled Novel in Progress

———————◆———————

The following three selections from James Welch's forthcoming novel, still in first draft stage, are printed here for the first time. The novel, which is presently untitled, concerns the Pikunis, the southernmost Blackfeet tribe and the one found in Montana today, during the years 1868-1870. Pressured by white (or Napikwans) cattlemen, the Montana territorial governor called on the military to subdue the Indians. Welch writes: "The Pikunis felt this pressure and knew something big was coming. And it came in the form of a massacre (the Baker Massacre or Massacre on the Marias) in January of 1870. 173 Pikunis were killed, mostly women and children. As a result of this massacre, the Blackfeet lay down their arms and never fought the whites again. The novel goes on after the massacre, but the massacre itself is pretty much the crisis point." Welch adds: "My main point in writing this book is to present the Blackfeet way of life—daily life, hunting, raiding, ceremonies, mores, beliefs, preparing hides and food—before the whites made real inroads into their culture. The Indians had a different reality and I try to present that."

◆

Fools Crow squeezed the trigger and quickly pumped another shell into the chamber, but there was no need. The white bighead collapsed where he had stood, then rolled over and off the narrow granite ledge.

He hit the long slide of scree at the top and slid all the way to the bottom. The report of the shot echoed in the high bowl, followed by the harsh slide of thin jagged shale. Then it was quiet. From this distance the white animal looked like a piece of summer snow. Fools Crow stood up and flexed his legs. He had been stalking the animal for most of the morning and his body was stiff. He sighed and looked around at the gray mountains. He hadn't known how good it would be for him and Killdeer to get away from the camp of the Lone Eaters. The visit by the seizers had only heightened a tension that had existed since the sun dance encampment. So many Napikwans, closing in all the time, had made the people feel that their time and place on the plains was jeopardized. Lately their only contacts with white people had brought bad news. It saddened them that Mountain Chief, one of the great leaders, was now on the run. It angered them to think that the seizers thought they could control Owl Child, as one hobbles a horse that has a tendency to wander. Now the seizers were determined that the leader pay for the crimes of another. This was like shooting a gopher because another had bit a child's finger. A war with the Napikwans seemed unavoidable and so Fools Crow was glad to come to the Backbone to clean his mind, to renew his spirit. When he and Killdeer returned to their people, he would be ready to fight for the hunting ranges that belonged to the Pikunis.

They had been in the mountains for eighteen sleeps and now the moon was approaching the time of the first frost on the plains. In the mountains the aspen had already turned a faint yellow. Fools Crow thought another ten sleeps would bring Cold Maker stirring from his lodge in the Always Winter Land. He was not afraid of Cold Maker, for he had made his offering soon after returning from the war against the Crows. He and Otter Child and Eagle Ribs had left camp before dawn one morning and ridden all that day to a sandy creek on the other side of the Medicine Line. There they killed and skinned three prairie hens and threw the pelts into a fire. Then they placed six prime blackhorn hides in the notch of a young cottonwood. They built up the fire and let it die down to a bed of red coals in the gathering dusk. As they rode back to camp in the starry night, they sang of their sacrifice and prayed that Cold Maker would find the robes adequate to clothe his daughters. The thought of them shivering in their bird skins in that Always Winter Land filled the warriors with pity. The coals would provide eyes for them to look down on the Pikunis and intercede on their behalf if Cold Maker became angry this winter. As they guided themselves to camp by the slender moonlit outlines of the Sweetgrass Hills, they suddenly felt an icy wind on their backs and they knew that Cold Maker had come to claim their offerings.

Fools Crow took off his shirt and sat down on the trail. It was just wide enough for him to stretch out his legs. He leaned back into a shallow crevice, into the shade and closed his eyes. He should get down to his animal, but the sun was warm and he felt sleepy. He would rest for a moment.

He awoke to the sound of laughter. He sat up quickly and bumped his head on a jutting rock. "Oh," he said, "Oh!" The laughter grew louder. He wiped away the tears. To the west he could see sun returning to his home. He scrambled to his feet and picked up his rifle. "Who is it?" he said. "Who laughs at me whem I am in such pain?" He spun around and lifted the rifle.

"Easy, brother," croaked Raven. "I was only laughing at what is going on below. Have a look."

Fools Crow leaned over the ledge. At the bottom of the scree he saw a large black shadow haloed with silver. Just before it entered the timber he caught a glimpse of white hair.

"Ah, ah," Raven laughed. "Ah, ah. That one is a thief. Look at him, as if he couldn't hunt for himself."

Fools Crow heard the animal crashing through the timber. He turned to Raven: "Why didn't you warn me sooner?"

"You think I haven't anything better to do, foolish man? I have to hunt for my wives! All day they pester me about not providing for them." Raven smiled. "As a matter of fact, I was just about to fly down there and take a piece for myself , but real-bear beat me to it."

"I stalked the white bighead all morning,"said Fools Crow bitterly. "I thought to lie my head on his white fur this winter. Now I have nothing."

"Now, now. Why is it you nothing-men think only of yourselves? Look at it his way—you have made a great sacrifice to real-bear. He will not forget. Besides, he makes your power-animal look like the turnip."

"You speak the truth," admitted Fools Crow. "Real-bear's power is the greatest of all the four-leggeds. He is a relative of the Pikunis. Still, I wish he hadn't chosen this one."

"The greater the sacrifice the greater the reward." Raven hopped down onto a ledge at shoulder-level. He ruffled his feathers and shit. He cocked his head and looked out across the bowl toward Rising Wolf. "I have come to speak to you about another matter."

Fools Crow was surprised to see that Raven's whiskers were white like those of an old coyote. But his eyes were dark and lively. The feet that curled over the edge of rock were black and tough. Fools Crow blinked as though his eyes played tricks on him. When he looked again he saw a thin band of silver around one of Raven's ankles. A pale blue stone caught the last of sun's light.

"Nice, isn't it? Not long ago I flew down to the Always Summer land to visit with my brothers there. One of them had taken this from the Many Bracelets. It has great power, Fools Crow. Now I see farther than ever."

"You know my new name?"

Raven laughed softly. "When I was flying home I decided to stop and see how the Crows were faring. I'm not too fond of the men, but the women enjoy my company. They give me lots to eat and they are nice to behold when one's eyes are sore with the wind. There is something about Crow women that makes me think of my youth..."

"You saw our war party attack the camp of Yellow Eyes!"

"Oh, yes. You killed twenty-three men. Alas, you also killed six women and one child."Raven sighed. "Such is war..."

"Then you saw me kill the two warriors!" Fools Crow exclaimed.

Raven reached down and picked at the silver bracelet. It jingled on the rock, the tiny sound echoing around the basin. "I don't think you fooled him, do you—the one you got your name for?"

Fools Crow felt his face grow hot with shame. "I tripped," he said weakly. "It was an accident. I thought I had been shot."

Raven laughed at the young man's discomfort. "Ah, but you see how it turns out? The people don't know that and so they speak your name with awe and admiration. It makes them feel good that one so brave walks among them. It increases the Pikuni's power. I'll never tell."

Both man and bird were silent for a moment, watching sun slip behind the Backbone. The heat from the rocks behind them warmed their backsides.

"Your long-ago people believed that Napi, who created them and gave them life and death, lives among these mountains, that he retired here after his work was completed."

"Yes," said Fools Crow. "My grandfather said that Old Man—and

Old Woman—still live in that place that gives life to Old Man River across the Medicine Line. He said that one can still see Napi's gambling place up there."

"He was a gambler, all right. After he made the first two-leggeds, he and Old Woman decided to gamble to see if your kind should live forever." Raven puffed himself up. "I was there. He picked up a buffalo chip and said 'I will throw this into the lake and if it floats, the people will die for four days, then return. If it sinks, they will die forever.' So saying, he threw the chip out as far as he could and it floated. But Old Woman, who was something of a gambler too, said, 'No, let me. I will throw this rock into the water. That will determine the people's fate.' The rock sank, and so you people die forever. Even Napi couldn't control his woman," Raven said sadly.

"But good came of it. Now people take care of themselves. And when they die, others feel sorry for them. It would be sad to die and think that nobody pities you."

"Did your grandfather tell you that?"

"He was a wise man."

"Not always," laughed Raven. "I knew him when he was a youth. Wild and reckless that one. Of course, he was poor—he was the poorest one of the Black Doors. That could account for some of the things he did to gain fame and wealth. I often wonder what would have become of him if I had not helped him..." Raven had a faraway look in his eyes. Then he shook his head. "But that is not what I wish to talk to you about.

"You see, seven, eight moons ago I became aware of an evil presence here in the Backbone. At first, I must admit, I didn't think of it as such. During my hunts I began to notice a lot of dead animals— real-bears, their cousins, the sticky mouths, long-tails, real-dogs, wags-his-tails, even the flyers, white head and Peta—in the beginning, I thought Sun Chief had chosen to smile on his poor relative. I brought the meat home to my wives and we gorged ourselves. Unlike you two-leggeds, we ravens prefer the meat of the meat-eaters, has more tang. After several days, my wives became worried and asked me to find out what was the matter with these creatures that they couldn't hold onto life. I told them to shut-up and enjoy the bounty, but they persisted in their demands." Raven wiped his beak under his wing. "By this time my belly was so big I couldn't fly very well. I begged my wives to let me rest up, but the cruel things pushed me out of the tree and said I couldn't come home until I had solved this riddle.

"Well, although my guts were aching with surfeit, I began to scout around, and it didn't take me long. The second day out I came upon a clearing filled with berries. There, in the center, a large real-bear was stripping the bushes into his mouth. It was disgusting the way his muzzle was covered with purple juice, but I decided to ask him if he knew what was going on. Just as I began my descent he stood up quickly and looked around. As you know, the real-bear has weak eyes but his nose is keen. He began sniffing the air, and that's when the Napikwan jumped up and shot him four times in the heart. That was natural. The two-leggeds are always killing for meat and hides. I settled in a tree and waited for the Napikwan to dress him out. I confess, the smell of blood had made me hungry again. I was anxious for some guts, but the Napikwan walked up to real-bear and shot him once more, this time in the ear. Then he swore in that peculiar language and walked away, leaving his kill.

"For three more sleeps I followed this strange Napikwan that leaves his meat. He killed a long-tail, a white head, three real-dogs and five wags-his-tails. He even tried to kill your brother, Wolverine, but I flew ahead and warned him. In anger, the Napikwan took a shot at me, scared the shit out of me, so I left. But for many moons now the hunter kills animals until they become scarce. I fear he will kill us all off if something isn't done.

"It was more than good fortune that brought you to me. I was flying over this bowl when my eyes caught sight of the white bighead lying at the bottom of the slide. I thought, 'Oh the crazy Napikwan kills another of my brothers.' You see, I have become afraid even to go down and pick carcasses. Look how skinny I have become. My wives call me coward and pick on me at home. Then I saw you up here, sleeping in the warm sun, and I knew Sun Chief had sent you."

Fools Crow frowned. He looked at Raven and saw that it was true that raven had become thin and ragged. Now his eyes didn't look so sharp and he seemed much older than that time he had led Fools Crow to the trapped wolverine. He pitied the old bird. "What can I do?" he said.

Without looking at his companion, Raven said, "You must kill him with your many-shots gun."

Fools Crow shuddered, as though the evening air had turned to winter. To kill a Napikwan was unthinkable! Had not the seizers warned the people against such ambitions? Hadn't his own father spoken against making trouble with them? He thought of Pete Owl Child and Fast Horse and their gang. They were different. He understood their hatred of the Napikwan. But in their blind ways they created trouble for their Pikuni relatives.

"I can't do it," he said, defeat coloring his voice.

"Would you have all your brothers killed off, then?"

"But surely real-bear can sneak up on him and..."

"This one is different. He is more animal than human. His ears can hear a leaf turn at five hundred paces. His eyes can spot a worm deep within the earth. They say he can smell a stone beyond the next ridge. No, we are no match for him—and that is why Sun Chief sent you to us. Only Fools Crow can kill this Napikwan."

"But how? Even now I tremble to think of this man. He will kill Fools Crow! Such a one would not release my spirit to the Shadowland. I would become a ghost. My people would grieve."

"But that is why Napi decided you would die forever—so your people would cry and mourn your loss." Raven smiled wryly. Then his eyes glittered with tears. "I thought Fools Crow was a man but now I see I was wrong. He would see his brothers, the four-leggeds and the flyers, perish and not put up a fight. He would allow his people to mourn the passing of their little brothers and starve for want of meat. He would rather his unborn child..."

"No, no, do not go on, Raven! Do not speak of such things. It was a selfish coward's heart that made me tremble with fear when I learned of Sun Chief's desire that I be the instrument of this Napikwan's destruction." Fools Crow brushed away a tear. "I will kill this one who destroys life so easily."

Raven looked at him shrewdly. "If your heart is not in this..."

"Now I hate him as I feared him before. I will kill him with a good heart. Fools Crow will put an end to this evil one."

Raven laughed. "Don't overdo it. You will need your strength for the accomplishment of this deed." He strutted back and forth on the ledge. "Such a brave one! A minute ago he is weeping with fear, and now he will rid the world of all evil!" he teased. Fools Crow could see his friend's spirits rise. He too began to laugh and the sound of their laughter travelled far in the approaching dusk. Killdeer, stirring, the berry soup in the valley below, heard the laughter and a smile lit her face.

That night Raven visited the dreaming place of the Napikwan. The low log-and-mud cabin was small. He pulled down on the rawhide string on the outside of the door. The latch inside popped up and the door swung open just wide enough for the ugly bird to waddle through. Across the room he could see coals smouldering in a rock fireplace. The inside of the cabin smelled of smoke and rancid grease and Napikwan's sour body. The grease smell sharpened Raven's appetite but he kept his mind on his work. He hopped up on a short bedpost at the man's feet. His eyes had become adjusted completely to the dark windowless room. He could see the big white feet pointing up at the bottom of the robe. There were three toes missing from the left one. Raven flapped his wings and flew as lightly as he could to a head post. The draft his wings created made the Napikwan's hair flutter. He stopped in the middle of a snore and licked his lips twice, then the air rushed out of his mouth with a whistle.

From the post, Raven could see this strange man who leaves his kills, and it was not a bad face in repose. The nose was long and sculpted on the sides with shadows. The eyelashes were fine and curved, if a little crusty. The rest of the face was covered with curly hair, a shade darker than the straight sandy hair on the head. Raven looked the length of the body. The white feet were a long way away.

Now Raven leaned over and began to sing in a voice unlike his own. The notes were as sweet and strong as those of the yellowbreast, yet made no sound in the small dark room. The words entered the man's ears and caused him to stop snoring. The words told a story of a young Pikuni woman, lovely and graceful, a woman of such charms that made men mad with longing. He sang of her shiny hair that hung undone to the small of her back, of her breasts so pale and firm they reminded one of the snow-bird eggs, of the lean dark thighs that invited perfect union. Raven was beginning to enjoy his work. He sang of long, soothing fingers, of skin as smooth and cool as the wet fur of Otter, of eyes that made the female wags-his tail cover her own in shame. The room had become hot and Raven began to croak out his praises of her hips, her nose and toes, the delicate hair of her center. Raven stopped and wiped his sweaty brow with the leading edge of his wing. Then he leaned closer to the man's ear and whispered where he could find this desirable creature. Raven told him to be sure to wear his wolf headdress so that maiden wouldn't mistake him for another Napikwan. She was so lonely that she would fall in love with the first man she laid eyes on.

Raven flew down and waddled out of the cabin. He jumped up and caught the string in his beak and closed the door. Then he sighed, a long shuddering croak. He would fly directly home. He had been too long away from his wives.

◆

Sun had cleared a small ridge to the southeast and was burning off the last of the groundfog when Killdeer finished washing the berry pot, the bowls and horn spoons. She sat back on her heels and watched the underwater swimmer that had stationed himself in an eddy behind a yellow rock. He would drift to the edge of the current, float downstream a short ways, then return with a wag of his tail. The day before she had tossed him a couple of yellowwings and he had darted up, his body splashing silver in the sun, to devour the insects. She had been tempted for three days now to catch him and taste of his flesh. Her own people scorned those who ate the underwater swimmers, but she had a cousin who had married into the Fish Eaters band of the Kainah and he had become fond of the silver creatures. He said they tasted like the breast meat of the young prairie hen. She wiped her wet hands on the hem of her dress and smiled. Today she would make a bone hook. She would catch him and cook him for Fools Crow. In the solitude of the Backbone they would tast the flesh of this silver one together.

She carried her dishes up the gentle incline to the lodge. The small meadow was filled with wind flowers, bear grass and lupine. The dry odor of juniper came with a small breeze. Downstream the thickets of chokecherry bushes glistened with the purple fruit, Killdeer felt her baby move inside her and she placed her hand on the slight roundness of her abdomen and crooned, "Be still, butterfly, the mighty hunter sleeps." Then she slipped into the bundles of dried roots, and picked up her beadwork and ducked quietly through the entrance again. She walked downstream a hundred paces to her favorite sitting spot, a grassy knoll beneath a tall fir that grew apart from the forest. She sat with her legs tucked under her and looked at the tiny moccasins. She had finished the yellow butterfly on one of them. She held the soft sole against her cheek. It was made of the softest elkskin. Fools Crow had shot a calf and she had spent several days tanning it. After cutting out the moccasins she had rolled the skin and tucked it away. It would yield more moccasins as the boy grew.

She looked back at the lodge. She was glad that Fools Crow had gone back to sleep after their morning meal. He had tossed and turned all night as though tormented by bad dreams.

Fools Crow got up when he could hear his wife's footsteps no longer. He put on his leggings, picked up his rifle and peeked out the door. When she had settled herself under the big fir tree, he hurried out and around the other side of the lodge. He had tethered the horses a good way upstream, out of sight. He trotted the few paces to the edge of the timber. Once in, he began to circle higher until he came to a patch of bushes a little above the top of the fir tree. From here he could see both upstream and downstream and the hillside across the meadow. He had wanted to warn Killdeer but Raven had said not to alarm her, for she would give away the trick by her actions. As he squatted behind a red bush he looked down at the back of his wife. She had grown more beautiful in the days since their marriage. Fools Crow didn't understand it, but her beauty had to do with the way she moved, the way she walked, even the way she sat. Her face and body had not changed, except for the slight swelling of her tummy—maybe that was it. He had seen women who were with child become serene, more womanly, more desirable. But they also became heavier, more centered on the ground as though to move would break some tie with mother earth's spirit. Killdeer was light and swift, as graceful as the antelope in her stride. Her body was still firm and yielding, her arms and legs those of the young girl, her hips wide and strong. When he watched her bathe in the stream, Fools Crow knew that he was married to a woman who turned other men's heads. Now he felt ashamed that it would be this beauty that would spring the trap.

Just before mid-day Fools Crow saw the Napikwan approach from upstream. He walked unhurriedly, without fear. He walked straight to the lodge and pushed back the flap with his gun barrel. He knelt and looked inside. Then he stood and looked first upstream, then across, then down. He was the biggest man Fools Crow had ever seen. In his fringed jacket and leggings, with his sandy beard and hair, he reminded Fools Crow of a molting blackhorn bull, half in and half out of his winter coat. His dark eyes stopped and Fools Crow knew he had spotted Killdeer. He stood still for a moment, then he walked back to the edge of the timber. From his vantage point Fools Crow could not see the man's upper body, but by laying his chin on the ground beside him he could see the long striding legs moving silently toward him. Then the legs stopped and spread slightly. The gun butt rested on the ground between them. Fools Crow grew frightened for Killdeer. Suppose Raven was wrong. Suppose the Napikwan's heart was not filled with lust, but instead, hatred. He had killed many animals for no reason; suppose now he wished to kill a human? Fools Crow glanced at Killdeer. She sat gracefully, her slim back bent over her beadwork. Then he looked back at the legs. The rifle butt had disappeared. The legs had shifted, so that the left one was now pointed toward Killdeer. The Napikwan was perhaps thirty paces below and to the right of Fools Crow. In the dry hot air, the warrior could hear the Napikwan's breathing. There was a hard edge to it as though the man had the winter sickness.

Fools Crow knew that the trick had gone wrong. The Napikwan was truly more animal than human. He had sensed the trap and now he was silently taunting Fools Crow to come out of hiding. Of course— he had looked into the lodge and seen the warrior's possessions. Raven had told him in his dream that Killdeer was alone. Now he was using Killdeer, the threat of harm, to make Fools Crow come out of hiding. Oh, thought the warrior, oh, not only is the Napikwan stronger, but he is smarter than Fools Crow as well. He began to tremble with fear. He wanted to shout to Killdeer to run, but the man was in easy range to drop her with one shot, should she move. Fools Crow lifted his rifle. His only chance was to shoot the man's legs out from under him. But as he sighted down the barrel, the legs moved back behind the trunk of a pine. Fools Crow lifted his head, then sat up slowly. He wiped his damp palms on his leggings. The big Napikwan is more than animal, he thought. He is a spirit who sees without seeing. Again Fools Crow wiped his palms on his leggings, but this time they weren't damp. Nor were his hands trembling. He was not afraid.

He stood, crouching, glancing about. There was a tree on the edge of the brushy clearing. If he could reach that he would have a better angle with which to get off a killing shot. The sun was hot on his bare back and sweat trickled down his ribs. Then he was running, dodging the red bushes, trying to see both the Napikwan and the ground before him. Suddenly he heard a boom! And he fell to the ground. He lifted his head, spitting dirt, and saw a fresh chip in the tree that had been his goal. He panicked. His only thought was to get to Killdeer before the Napikwan decided to kill her. He was running down the slope, shouting at her to get away, but she didn't move. She watched him come near with a questioning look in her eyes. Her mouth was open as though she were about to speak. The next shot lifted Fools Crow off his feet and spun him around. He came down hard on his back and slid until he was stopped by a small pine. He pulled himself up and leaned back against the tree. His breathing was raspy. Then at the same time he heard Killdeer scream and the Napikwan shout something in a slow singing voice. He continued to sing as though he were boasting, mocking the Pikuni warrior. Fools Crow looked at his shoulder. A piece of flesh had been blasted away just below the shoulder bone. It was matted with dirt and grass. His rifle lay on the slope two body lengths away. He heard the Napikwan laugh and then another boom. The small tree snapped in two above his head. Fools Crow leaned back and breathed deeply and he saw a red wall come up behind his eyes. He felt sick and weak. He closed his eyes and called out to Sun Chief, to Wolverine, his power animal to give him strength, to let him die with honor. Slowly, almost silently, a sound entered his ears. As the sound increased in volume, the red wall behind his eyes receded. Now he saw the slope clearly, the red bushes, the slender blonde grasses—and his gun. The sound was in his head and in the small meadow surrounded by the great mountains of the Backbone. The sound flowed through his body and he felt the strength of its music in his limbs, in his hands, in his guts, in his chest. He sprang to a crouch, then made a dive for his weapon. A boom kicked up a patch of duff inches from his head. But the music had reached his heart. The weapon was in his hands, against his cheek, and he watched the greased shooter leave his rifle and he watched it travel throught the air, between the trees, and he saw it enter the Napikwan's forehead above the startled eyes, below the wolfskin headdress, and he squatted and watched the head jerk back, then the body, until it landed with a quivering shudder in the bear grass, the lupine, the wind flowers. Then the sound was no more. Fools Crow's death song had ended.

◆

"How did you become a many-faces man, Mik-api?" White Man's Dog said this as he helped his friend prepare the sweat lodge. Otter Child had asked Mik-api to help him with a dream that had been troubling him for several sleeps. So Mik-api had agreed to a sweat ceremony with the youth.

Mik-api tugged one of the blackened hides over the willow frame. He caught his breath and began: "It was many moons ago. I am now of sixty-seven winters but I wasn't always old. Once when I was a young man, not much older than you, I had my heart set on becoming a great warrior and a rich man. There were very few of the Napikwans in those days. It was when I was born that the first Old Man Persons appeared in this country. They came up the Two Medicine Lodges not far from here and first they tried to trade with our people, then they tried to kill us. We grew frightened of their firesticks and ran away and then they ran away. It wasn't long after that, that others came into our country. Most of them stayed in the mountains and they trapped the fine-furred animals—the woodbiters, the mink, the muskrat, and otter. I remember seeing them sometimes, but they didn't bother us and we didn't see them much. Many of them were as furry as the animals, but not so fine." Mik-api laughed. "They always stunk like mink. A few of our less fortunate girls went to live with them and we didn't see much of them after that. I think these men hated each other, for you never saw two of them together and our women who went with them became little more than slaves. I don't know what the trouble was but you never saw children around their dwellings." Mik-api shook his head sadly. "We at first thought these Napikwans were animals and incapable of reproducing with human beings. But they were intelligent in a cruel way . . .

"Now I forget my story. Ah yes, you ask me when I became one of the many-faces. It was in that season of the fallingleaves moon and I had been hunting in the mountains where the Shield Floated Away River begins. I had been lucky and as I packed out one late morning I had two elk and a small sticky-mouth, gutted and cleaned, across my pack horses. I had killed these animals because my family wanted a change from the real-meat. It was brushy all around there and so I was riding down the middle of the river, singing my victory song. Between my song and the noise the horses made over the rocks I didn't hear much else. But then I stopped to admire a grove of the small quaking trees. They had not yet lost their leaves and they were golden against the rock wall behind them. As I sat there in all that beauty I started to sing a song I had made up for my girlfriend, but I heard something else, a kind of a wail that reminded me of a puppy but I knew no dogs lived around there, so I guessed it must be a young coyote or wolf. I dismounted there in the water, for I had always wanted one of these creatures for a pet. I took my lariat and crept into the bushes but the wailing had stopped. I listened for a long time but it never started again. Just as I was about to leave I saw some broken grass at my feet. Further along I found the place where the thing had entered the brush. There was a trail of willows that did not stand straight. I took my knife in hand and followed the bent willows some ways away from the river. Then I saw something dark ahead and as I crept closer I could see that it was a man. He lay on his back, his head propped against a rock, a knife in his right hand. I was off to one side and I thought to sneak up and lift the man's hair. But then the man flopped his head in my direction and I saw who it was. It is Head Carrier, I cried out, for it was he who later became the great warrior of the ghost shirt. But he was a youth then, a year older than me. As I ran through the brush I saw him lift his head and knife at the same time; then he recognized me. Oh Spotted Weasel, he cried—for that was my name then—I am killed by the murderous Snakes. With that he closed his eyes and keeled over. I ran to him for I was sure he had passed to the Sand Hills. He had two broken-off arrows in him—one in his side and one in the guts. I pulled back his shirt and listened to his heart and I could hear a faint murmuring. Then I rolled him over on his side. The arrow in his ribs had passed through his body and the arrowhead was sticky with blood. I managed to tie my lariat around the shaft behind the arrowhead, and with a great deal of effort, pulled it through his body. But the arrow in his guts had not come through. I brought him water and made him drink but he couldn't take much. I bathed his wounds as best I could and I held him and cried. Along came dusk and he opened his eyes and said in a weak voice, Go away, Spotted Weasel, let me die like a warrior. And so, still weeping, I left him there and wandered back into the brush. I could hear his death song getting fainter behind me. I found a slough and sat with my head in my hands. All around me the green singers were tuning up. I had never liked frogs but as I cried I became aware of the beauty of their song. It filled me with so much sadness I thought my heart would break and I cried louder. Soon the biggest of the green persons came up to me and said, Why do you weep when all we mean to do is cheer you up? Are you not grateful to us? And so I told him about my friend, Head Carrier, who lay dying. He said, I understand how it is with friends. But you people sometimes play with us and kill us for no reason. You are very cruel to your brothers. And I cried, Oh, underwater swimmer, if you will help me I will tell my people to leave you alone. Never again will a Pikuni harm his little brother. So Frog signaled me to be patient and dived into the slough. He was gone for a long time. Seven Persons had begun to sink in the night sky when he came up again. He carried deep in his fat throat a ball of stinking green mud. He was exhausted and I helped him crawl out on the bank. After a while he said, I had to go to the home of the chief of the Underwater People. He was reluctant to help but after I told him your vow he gave this medicine to me. Now take it and smear it on the wounds of your friend.

I ran back to Head Carrier shouting and whooping for I knew he would be glad to see me. But when I got there he was cold and stiff and his eyes stared up at the stars. Now I knew he had gone to the Shadowland. Without much hope I smeared the stinking mud on his wounds, then fell into a deep sleep. A small time later I felt something cold on my face and when I woke up there stood Head Carrier, dripping wet. Wake up, you nothing-man, he said to me, you have slept half the morning and I have already been swimming. I sat up and looked at him for I was sure he was a ghost who had come to torture me. But he said, "When I woke up this morning I had the strangest feeling that I had gone to a place that no man returns from. I dreamed that I had been killed by the Snakes. And when I looked down I had some stinking stuff all over my body and so I went down to the river and washed it off." I looked at his body and there was not a mark on it.

Later, at a ceremonial involving many of our people, I told this story to my mother's sister, who was a healing woman among the Never Laughs band. Foolish young man, why didn't you tell me of his sooner? she said. Now I will teach you all the ways of healing for you are truly chosen. So I became a many-faces and so I am."

◆

It was a sunny windless day and the seven children pulling their buffalo rib sleds to a steep hill beyond the horse herds talked and teased each other. The two girls, at twelve winters, were the oldest. They had been sent to keep an eye on the younger ones, but they were not happy, for the five boys made jokes about the size of their breasts and the skinnyness of their legs. One Spot, in particular, was cruel to them. He liked these times when he didn't have to follow his older brother around, and so he bullied the younger boys and made the girls chase him. He boasted of his hunting skill and tried to rub snow in another boy's face. When one of the girls hit him with a small skin of pemmican, it stung his cheek but he didn't cry. He called the girl Skinny Weasel and he liked her, although she was a year older than he was. She liked One Spot's brother, Good Young Man, but he was more interested in hunting than girls. He was off hunting the bighorns with Fools Crow now in the foothills of the Backbone. They would be gone for two or three sleeps. One Spot had been jealous of Good Young Man's fortune, but Fools Crow had promised him a set of horns. He picked up a handful of snow and threw it at Skinny Weasel. His cheek stung but he liked her.

None of them noticed the wolf that had emerged from behind a clump of drifted-over greasewood until he was fifty paces to the side of them. He was large and gray and his eyes were golden in the brilliant sun. Snow clung to one side of him as though he had been lying down. As he walked, his tail drooped and dragged on the deep snow and a sound, somewhere between a growl and a grunt, came up from his chest.

It was this sound that Skinny Weasel's girlfriend heard, and when she looked over she saw the animal's gait was shaky and listed to one side. He had his head down, but she noticed his tongue hanging almost to the snow. Then she saw the whiteness around his mouth and she thought he had been eating snow. Her first impulse was to turn and run, but then the wolf began to veer away from them. She watched him out of the corner of her eye as the wolf circled behind them. Then she said something to Skinny Weasel in a low voice and the girls stopped and turned. It was at this point that one of the boys let out a cry of fear, for he had just seen the wolf.

The wolf looked up at them and coughed and bared his fangs, making chewing motions as though he were trying to rid himself of a bone or hairball. He watched listlessly as the children ran, all but One Spot, who stood in the deep snow with his hands on his hips. He taunted the bigmouth with a war song that he had learned from Fools Crow.

The other children stopped near the base of the big hill and turned to watch. The wolf covered the thirty paces with such speed that they didn't have a chance to cry out a warning. By the time One Spot had turned to run, the wolf was upon him, knocking him face-down in the snow, standing over him, growling, the hair on his back standing up and shining in the sunlight. The children screamed as they watched the wolf attack the bundled-up child as he tried to crawl away. He struck repeatedly at the blanket, his low growl now a roar of fury. At last he found One Spot's head and sank his fangs into the exposed skin behind the ear. The child screamed in pain and turned over, only to feel a fang knock against his cheek bone, opening it up. Then the fangs were twisting and pulling at the cheek, gnashing into the soft flesh. One Spot felt the wetness and the hot breath. He saw for one brief instant the yellow eye and the laid-back ear—then he sank into the red darkness and deep snow.

Skinny Weasel was crying as she watched the wolf stagger away. In his charge and attack he had used up the last of his energy. Now his throat was swollen shut and the saliva hung in long strands from his mouth. He began a wide circle, always veering to his right, his eyes now seeing nothing, his breath coming in harsh barks, his tongue and tail once again hanging and dragging on the snow. Skinny Weasel watched him disappear behind a stand of willows near the river; then she ran to the limp, ragged form in the snow field. When she rolled him over, she bit her lips to keep from screaming. A flap of ragged skin lay back over One Spot's eye, exposing the clean white bone of his cheek. One ear lobe hung from a thin piece of skin and there was a large mat of blood in the hair. She thought she heard a rattle deep in the boy's throat. With a shudder, she placed the flap of skin down over the cheek bone. Then she and the others managed to lift him onto his sled. Skinny Weasel's girl friend covered him up with her own blanket. Then the two girls pulled the sled through the deep snow back toward camp. The sun was still high and the sweat was cool on the girls' bodies.

◆

By the time Fools Crow and Good Young Man got back from their hunting trip, four days later, One Spot was able to sit up and take some meat. But most of the time he lay in his robes and thought of the yellow eye and the laid-back ear, the harsh breath and the snapping teeth. Every time he closed his eyes, he saw the bounding wolf and he cried out in his weakness and pain. Heavy Shield Woman had slept little, despite the fact that Killdeer and another woman had attempted to take over the nursing of her son. Now she sat in a listless trance and thought of the many things that had happened to her family. She didn't really think, but images of White Quiver and Killdeer and Good Young Man entered her head and they all seemed far away, as though she had lost them all. Even when she looked down at One Spot, in one of his rare moments of peace, she saw the black pitchy substance that held his cheek in place and she thought that he had gone away from her too. Only Killdeer was there to talk with, but Heavy Shield Woman didn't talk. She answered questions without elaboration and she didn't volunteer any conversation. In some ways, she felt a lingering guilt (she had felt for some time) about her role as medicine woman at the Sun Dance ceremonies. She thought she could not be a virtuous woman, for she felt no happiness or peace since her husband was returned to her. Her virtue (if that was what it was) resulted from a drab emptiness in her life, a day to day barrenness of spirit relieved only by moments of pleasure at the antics of her sons and Killdeer's swelling belly. But these moments were short-lived and only increased her over-all sadness, as she thought of their futures, her own future. She knew she would never see White Quiver again and that thought almost gave her relief; but then she would think of the happiness they had shared, the times they had lain together, the pride in his eyes each time she delivered him a son, and she would become consumed with a restless fury. Many times she thought of going to Three Bears and telling him what was in her heart and renouncing her role as medicine woman. In her mind she had already done so. Now when the girls looked to her for guidance, she averted her eyes and said nothing. She began to avoid them, for she was sure they would see in her eyes what she felt in her heart.

But Fools Crow and Good Young Man did not know any of this as they rode into camp with the carcasses of two bighorns. True to his word Fools Crow had a set of horns tied to the frame of one of the pack horses. He rode first to his own lodge and dumped one of the bighorns in the snow beside the entrance. Then he led the other pack horse to Heavy Shield Woman's lodge, kicking a black dog in the ribs when he became too curious. As he loosened the rawhide strings that held the animal down, Killdeer emerged from her mother's lodge. She came forward and squeezed his upper arm and smiled. She called to her brother, Good Young Man, who sat exhausted on his horse, ready to drive the pack horses back to the herd. Wearily, he rolled onto his belly and slid off the horse. He had planned to return to the camp in triumph because he had shot one of the bighorns with Fools Crow's rifle, but now he felt the stiffness in his legs and wanted only to lie down and sleep.

But Killdeer motioned him close, and then she told them about One Spot's encounter with the wolf. Even as she explained that he was all right, her voice shook and she looked at Fools Crow's feet. Good Young Man listened to his sister, first with fear, and then relief. He had forgotten about being tired, and when his sister paused, he ducked into the lodge.

Killdeer looked into her husband's eyes. "The children he was with think the wolf might have the whitemouth. They say he was acting funny, walking sideways in a big circle, his tail dragging in the snow. They think he had the foam on the mouth, but they couldn't tell if it was that, or if he was eating snow."

"Did he breathe different?"

"Skinny Weasel said it was like a harsh bark in his throat."

"Maybe," said Killdeer, but her voice was doubtful.

"Is your mother in the lodge?"

"She is out gathering firewood."

Fools Crow entered the lodge, with Killdeer right behind him. Good Young Man knelt beside his brother, holding his hand. One Spot looked at Fools Crow; then he grinned.

"I sang my war song," he said.

"But did you have your weapons?" Fools Crow got down on his knees and ruffled the boy's hair.

"No," the boy said sheepishly.

"Hai-ya! What warrior goes out empty-handed?"

"He would kill this wolf with his bare hands. He would be a great warrior," said Good Young Man with a smile.

"If I had my knife—"

"If he had his knife! Listen to him talk!" Fools Crow laughed. "And now you have your first battle wounds. Let me see." Fools Crow leaned over the boy's face. The patch of skin held by the black pitch looked a pale purple and was slightly swollen. He almost lost his whole cheek, thought Fools Crow. As it is, it will always be swollen and discolored, but it will at least be there. The earlobe was completely bitten off and would cause no trouble. But behind the ear, in a patch of cut-off hair, there were several puncture wounds. The whole area was an angry red, except for the small white circles around each fang mark. These were draining, but the area was swollen and tender-looking. It scared Fools Crow to look at these wounds, but he didn't say anything.

"He has nightmares," said Killdeer. "He gets very little sleep because of them."

"Sleep-bringer will visit soon. All warriors have bad dreams after battle—they will pass." Fools Crow looked down at One Spot. "You must not think of this wolf as your enemy. He did only what wolves will do. The big-mouth is a sacred power-animal, and if he visits you in your dreams, it is only because he wishes to help you. Someday, he will become your secret helper."

"When I am old enough for my vision?"

"Yes. Then he will come to you and give you some of his secret medicine. But for now, you must think of him as your brother and treat him with great respect. Do you understand that?"

"But why did he attack me?"

"This one was—sick. I think he didn't know what he was doing. But wolves are unpredictable. It is best to leave them alone, even if they are our brothers—like the real-bear."

"Will I have a scar forever?"

"Do you remember the story of Poia—Scarface?"

"Yes. He came from Sun Chief and instructed our people in the Sun Dance. Afterward, Sun Chief made him a star in the sky, just like his father, Morning Star."

"But before all that, he was a boy just like you, with a scar on his face—"

"But the people laughed at him and scorned him!"

"In those days, the people were not wise. Now we honor Poia. Of all the Above Ones, he is most like us, and so you must think of your scar as a mark of honor. You will wear it proudly and the people will be proud of you. And they will think highly of you because you did not kill your brother, the wolf." Fools Crow laughed. "We will tell them you took pity on this big mouth."

One Spot thought for a moment, his dark eyes narrowed and staring up at the point where the lodge-poles came together. He heard some children run by but he didn't envy them. Finally he said, "Yes, I took pity on my brother. But if I had my weapons, I surely would have killed him."

One Spot did not get over his dreams, but now instead of attacking him, the wolf turned away or stopped, sometimes lifting his lip to growl, other times simply staring at the boy through golden eyes. But he always kept his distance and One Spot, in spite of his fear, began to look forward to the wolf's visits, for he was memorizing every aspect of the animal, from his silver-tipped fur to the way his long ears flickered when One Spot shouted at him. For seven sleeps he dreamed of the big-mouth and on the eighth day, he was well enough to walk down to the river to throw rocks. Good Young Man stayed with him, never leaving the lodge to play with friends or even to visit Killdeer and Fools Crow. Together, he and his mother had skinned and quartered the bighorn. The meat was strong but good and would last a long time. Heavy Shield Woman also seemed to be improving. For the first time in many sleeps she went to visit a friend who lived on the other side of camp. The friend was very glad to see her for she had been concerned about Heavy Shield Woman. They ate and talked until well after dark and the friend noticed that Heavy Shield Woman smiled and laughed more than she had in some time, and talked less about her bad fortune. When the friend's husband came home, with a fat blackhorn cow he had killed on the Cutbank, Heavy Shield Woman remembered that she had not fed One Spot and Good Young Man. She looked up at the stars as she hurried along the icy path to her lodge and the cold air was fresh in her chest.

When she entered the lodge, Good Young Man looked up anxiously. He was kneeling by his brother's side. "One Spot seems to be sick again. He seems to have difficulty swallowing. He moves his jaws and is thirsty all the time but he can't drink."

Heavy Shield Woman ran to One Spot and sank to her knees. His forehead glistened in the firelight and his throat seemed to jump and quiver on its own. He looked up at her and his eyes were wide with fear. He tried to speak but the effort made him swallow and he cried out in pain. In panic he began to thrash around under the buffalo robe. Heavy Shield Woman held him and spoke soothing words to him, but he didn't seem to hear or know her.

"Good Young Man, put on the water to heat—build up the fire first—then run for Fools Crow and Killdeer. Run fast."

One Spot had quieted down a little, but when Heavy Shield Woman looked down at him, she saw the saliva bubbling around his mouth. His eyes were dark and unseeing.

When Good Young Man returned with Fools Crow and Killdeer, Heavy Shield Woman was mopping the sick boy's face with a cloth dampened in the warm water. Suddenly One Spot began to tremble violently and make noises in his throat. He tried to kick the robe off, but Fools Crow held his legs.

"It is the whitemouth," he said. "The wolf has infected him."

"Oh, I feared it. I knew it would happen. I saw it once as a girl. But we must do something!" Heavy Shield Woman moaned as she remembered how her girlfriend had died of a kit-fox bite. She had never forgotten it, and now she was seeing it again.

"'Killdeer! Hold his legs while I get Mik-api." But before he left, he glanced at One Spot's face and he shuddered.

Fools Crow was gone for what seemed like half the night. Killdeer helped her mother hold down the struggling boy. He did not recognize either of them, but the strange noise in his throat seemed a cry for help. Killdeer sank back on her heels once when her brother suddenly stopped and held himself rigid. She wiped the sweat from her forehead, and only then did she realize that she had been crying.

At last, Fools Crow entered the lodge. His chest was heaving and his face was crimson.

"Where's Mik-api?" Killdeer held her breath.

"I searched the camp—but he was not to be found."

He looked down and Heavy Shield Woman was looking up at him with a blankness in her eyes. He suddenly thought that he had not looked at her this way since he had married Killdeer—nor had she looked at him. But now this taboo did not matter.

"We need a green hide," he said. "Mik-api once told me how to do this."

Heavy Shield Woman looked down at her son who was beginning to stir again. A trickle of blood from the cresent scab on his cheek ran down his neck, she wiped the saliva from his mouth. "Morning Eagle has just returned from his hunt. He brought back a blackhorn."

Fools Crow ran across a small icy field to Morning Eagle's lodge. He told the hunter what he needed and the two men began to skin the blackhorn. They worked quickly, not caring if they punctured the skin or left too much meat on it.

When they finished, Fools Crow draped the skin over his shoulder and began to trot back to Heavy Shield Woman's lodge. He was surprised to see so many people standing around. They had been talking among themselves, but he hadn't heard a word.

Back in the lodge the two women undressed the violent boy while Fools Crow spread the green hide, skin side up, on the other side of the fire. Good Young Man helped him clear away the spot. Fools Crow clapped him on the shoulder and squeezed. Then he helped the women carry One Spot over to the hide. He was taken aback by the strength in the small body and he understood how much effort it had taken the women to hold him down. But they managed to lay him on the smooth cool skin, with his arms pinned to his sides, and roll him up. Only his head stuck out of the furry bundle. Killdeer looked down and could not believe that the contorted face, the white foamy mouth which uttered such strange harsh sounds, belonged to her younger brother. But she knew that when a bad spirit entered one's body, the body no longer belonged to the person but became the embodiment of that spirit. And so, as she looked at the face, she grew calm, for she felt that now the spirit had been trapped, her husband would drive it away with the medicine he learned from Mik-api. She helped her mother to the far side of the fire and squatted to watch.

◆

Fools Crow, who had stopped by his lodge for his parfleche of medicines, took out a small bundle of sweetgrass and threw some into the fire. Then he lit braids and purified both the out-of-his-mind boy and himself. He began to chant in a steady rhythm that matched his own heartbeat. As he chanted he passed his hands over the boy. His eyes were closed and the steady rhythm of his voice seemed to place the boy under a spell. One Spot had stopped struggling and the noise in his throat became less a cry of fear and pain. Then Fools Crow removed a burning stick from the fire and touched it against the furry hide. There was a hiss and the lodge was suddenly filled with the stink of burning hair. Heavy Shield Woman started, but Killdeer held her close. Still chanting, Fools Crow burned off more of the curly hair. He did this several times until the hair was black and crinkly, then he turned the boy over, and the movement made One Spot cry out. But Fools Crow began to pass the burning stick over the green robe, lighting long strips of hair and the smell made Killdeer feel faint. She looked beyond her mother to Good Young Man, but he was watching intently, mesmerized by the moving stick of fire. Again Fools Crow turned the boy over until he was lying on his stomach. The boy made no sound and Killdeer became frightened. But when she saw his eyes flicker, she let out a deep breath.

Once Fools Crow stopped to wipe One Spot's sweat-drenched head. He looked into the boy's eyes, but they were opaque and without recognition. Then he turned him again and burned off the last of the hair.

When he finished, Fools Crow threw a bundle of sage onto the fire to purify the air. As he did this he said a prayer to the Above Ones and to the Medicine Wolf to take pity on the boy and to restore him to health. Then he instructed the women to unwrap him and bathe him with warm water. While they did this, he took some sticky-root and tastes-dry and ground it up into a paste.

The women placed the small limp body on a robe and Fools Crow swabbed the paste on the boy's throat. They covered him with another robe.

Fools Crow sent the two women back to his own lodge, there to prepare some broth and meat. He said he would send Good Young Man to fetch them when they were needed. Heavy Shield Woman was reluctant to leave, but Killdeer talked her out of the lodge. The sudden draft of cold air swirled through the lodge and dried the sweat on Fools Crow's face. The lodge smelled of burnt hair and sage and sticky-root.

Good Young Man built up the fire and gave Fools Crow a drink of water. He dipped another cupful and looked questioningly at his younger brother, but the medicine man shook his head and motioned the youth to sit on the other side of the fire.

For the rest of that night Fools Crow beat on his small drum, which was nothing more than a piece of tough neck hide stretched over a willow frame. His stick was made of ash, rounded at one end and feathered at the other. He accompanied the slow beat with a monotonous song, and in spite of his fascination, Good Young Man eventually fell asleep. Four times before dawn he was awakened by a shrill whistle—short, furious blasts—and started to his feet to see Fools Crow blowing his eagle-bone pipe over the length of the still form of One Spot. Then he would watch for a while before drifting off again.

Sometime after first light, he awoke and it was quiet. He threw back the robe and sat up. Fools Crow still knelt beside his brother, but now he was hunched over, his head down. Good Young Man watched his broad back move up and down with his breathing. Then he slid from beneath the robe and tended to the fire. It was nearly out, but he coaxed a flame out of some dry twigs. When he had the fire crackling, he crept around and looked down at the face of his younger brother. In the half-light of dawn, the face looked pale and shiny, like the back-fat of a blackhorn. Only the skin on the cheek that had been torn away had some color. It was a dull purple, fading to bright pink along the scar. Good Young Man got down on all fours and looked closer. He looked at the chest beneath the robe. Nothing moved. He became frightened and in his fear, he blew on the face. The eyes seemed to move beneath the lids. He blew again, and this time the eyes opened and the brows came down in irritation.

"James Welch:
A Bibliography"

————————◆————————

Ronald E. McFarland

The following is as complete a bibliography of James Welch's works and of the critical and scholarly materials pertaining to the works as I could compile. For the magazine and anthology listings of Welch's poems, I am especially indebted to Angeline Jacobson's listings, *Contemporary Native American Literature* (Methuen, New Jersey: Scarecrow, 1977), pp. 115-120. The foundation of my lists of critical and scholarly work is the bibliography in Peter Wild's pamphlet on Welch published in the Western Writers Series (Boise: Boise State University Press, 1983), pp. 47-49. In listing certain reviews as "Selected," I have distinguished generally those which might be considered "review essays" and those by reviewers with established reputations. I have not culled out negative reviews, but I have as a rule relegated the "anonymous" review to the "Other Reviews" section, along with the brief notice.

Ron McFarland

Books

The Death of Jim Loney. New York: Harper and Row, 1979.

Riding the Earthboy 40. New York: World, 1971. Revised edition, New York: Harper and Row, 1976.

Winter in the Blood. New York: Harper and Row, 1974.

Selections from Fiction in Progress

"The Only Good Indian: Section I of a Novel in Progress." *South Dakota Review,* 9 (Summer 1971), 49-74. Portion of an early version of *Winter in the Blood.*

"Her Best Moments." *Rocky Mountain Magazine,* 1 (July/August 1979) 34-43. Selections from *The Death of Jim Loney.*

Welch's Poetry

Anthologies

Carroll, Paul, ed. *Young American Poets.* Chicago: Follett, 1968.
    "Blackfeet, Blood and Piegan Hunters"
    "Christmas Comes to Moccasin Flat"
    "D-Y Bar"
    "In My First Hard Springtime"
    "Montana, Nothing Like Boston"
    "Spring for All Seasons"
    "Winter Indian"
    "Wolf Song, the Rain"
    "The Wrath of Lester Lame Bull"

David, Jay, ed. *The American Indian, The First Victim.* New York: Morrow, 1972.
    "Christmas Comes to Moccasin Flat"

Dodge, Robert K. and Joseph B. McCullough, eds. *Voices from Wah'kon-tah.* New York: International, 1974. 2nd ed., 1976.
    "Dreaming Winter"
    "Harlem, Montana"
    "Just Off the Reservation"
    "The Man from Washington"
    "One More Time"

Haslam, Gerald W., ed. *Forgotten Pages of American Literature.* New York: Houghton-Mifflin, 1970.
    "Grandma's Man"
    "Snow Country Weavers"
    "Surviving"

Lowenfels, Walter, ed. *From the Belly of the Shark.* New York: Vintage, 1973.
  "Getting Things Straight"

Milton, John R., ed. *The American Indian Speaks.* Vermillion: University of South
  Dakota, 1969. Special issue of *South Dakota Review,* 7 (Summer 1969).
  "Birth on Range 18"
  "Grandma's Man"
  "Legends Like This"
  "The Man from Washington"
  "One More Time"
  "Snow Country Weavers"
  "Surviving"

Momaday, N. Scott, ed. *American Indian Authors.* New York: Houghton-Mifflin, 1972.
  "The Man from Washington"

Niatum, Duane, ed. *Carriers of the Dream Wheel.* New York: Harper and Row, 1975.
  "Across to the Peloponnese"
  "Arizona Highways"
  "Blue Like Death"
  "Christmas Comes to Moccasin Flat"
  "D-Y Bar"
  "Directions to the Nomad"
  "Going to Remake This World"
  "Harlem, Montana"
  "In My First Hard Springtime"
  "Magic Fox"
  "The Man from Washington"
  "Please Forward"
  "The Renegade Wants Words"
  "Snow Country Weavers"
  "Surviving"
  "Verifying the Dead"
  "Why I Didn't Go to Delphi"

Sanders, Thomas and Walter W. Peek, eds. *Literature of the American Indian.* Beverly
Hills, California: Glencoe, 1973.
  "In My Lifetime"
  "Snow Country Weavers"
  "The Versatile Historian"

Turner, Frederick W., III, ed. *The Portable North American Reader.* New York: Viking,
1974.
  "Christmas Comes to Moccasin Flat"
  "In My Lifetime"
  "Surviving"

Tvedten, Benet, ed. *An American Indian Anthology.* Marvin, South Dakota: Blue Cloud
Abbey, 1971.
  "The Man from Washington"

Witt, Shirley H. and Stan Steiner, eds. *The Way: An Anthology of American Indian Literature.* New York: Vintage, 1972.
"The Man from Washington"

Magazines

"Christmas Comes to Moccasin Flat"
"In My First Hard Springtime"
Poetry Northwest, 8 (Spring 1967), 34-5.

"Dancing Man"
Harper's Bazaar, 103 (August 1970), 156.

"Dreaming Winter"
"Harlem, Montana"
Poetry, 112 (April 1968), 16, 17-18.

"The Only Bar in Dixon."
New Yorker, 46 (October 10, 1970), 48.

General Studies Of Welch's Works

Bevis, Bill. "Dialogue with James Welch." *Northwest Review*, 20 (1982), 163-185.

Wild, Peter. *James Welch.* Boise: Boise State University Press, 1983.

Riding The Earthboy 40

Reviews and Essays

Amanuddin, Syed. Review. *World Literature Today*, *51* (Winter 1977), 142.

Anonymous. Review. *Choice*, *13* (April 1976), 228.

Holland, Robert. Review. *Poetry*, *129* (February 1977), 285-295.

Kessler, Jascha. Review. *Saturday Review*, *54* (October 2, 1971), 50.

Lincoln, Kenneth. "Native American Literatures: 'old like hills, like stars." In *Three American Literatures.* Houston A. Baker, Jr., ed. New York: MLA, 1982. Pp. 140-161. Partially reprinted in this volume.

Stafford, William. Review. *Journal of Ethnic Studies*, 4 (Fall 1976), 107-108.

Velie, Alan R. "Blackfeet Surrealism: The Poetry of James Welch." In *Four American Indian Literary Masters.* Norman: University of Oklahoma Press, 1982. Pp. 65-90.

"James Welch's Poetry." *American Indian Culture and Research Journal*, 3 (1979), 19-38.

Winter In The Blood

Selected Reviews

Broyard, Anatole. *New York Times*, 124 (October 30, 1974), 43.

Gelfant, Blanche H. *Hudson Review*, 28 (Summer 1975), 309-312.

Gray, Paul. *Time*, 104 (December 9, 1974), 103-105.

Grossbardt, Andrew. *New Letters*, 41 (March 1975), 110.

Jefferson, Margo. *Newsweek*, 84 (November 11, 1974), 114-115.

Klein, Carol M. *Library Journal*, 99 (December 1, 1974), 3148.

Larson, Charles R. *New Republic*, 171 (December 14, 1974), 26-27.

Price, Reynolds. *New York Times Book Review*, (November 10, 1074), 1.

Reedy, Gerard. *America*, 132 (April 12, 1975), 306.

Sale, Roger. *New York Review of Books*, 21 (December 12, 1974), 18-22.

Urion, Celia. *Thoreau Journal Quarterly*, 9 (January 1977), 26-28.

Weeks, Edward. *Atlantic*, 235 (January 1975), 88.

Other Reviews

American West, 16 (May 1979), 48.
Best Sellers, 34 (January 15, 1975), 473.
Gargoyle, 17/18 (1982), 69.
Kirkus Reviews, 42 (October 15, 1974), 1121.
New Yorker, 50 (December 23, 1974), 84.
Publishers' Weekly, 206 (September 30, 1974), 52.
Saturday Review/World, 2 (December 14, 1974), 102.
Village Voice, 19 (October 24, 1974), 36.
Virginia Quarterly Review, 51 (Spring 1975), lii.

Essays

Barnett, Louise K. "Alienation and Ritual in *Winter in the Blood.*" *American Indian Quarterly*, 4 (May 1978), 123-30.

Barry, Nora Baker. "*Winter in the Blood* as Elegy." *American Indian Quarterly*, 4 (May 1978), 149-57.

Biedler, Peter G. "Animals and Human Development in the Contemporary American Indian Novel." *Western American Literature*, 14 (August 1979), 133-48.

Contributors

————————◆————————

Jack L. Davis is a professor of English at the University of Idaho. Part Cherokee on his father's side, he teaches Native American Literature courses and is completing a book tentatively entitled *"Civilizing the White Man."*

Robert Gish is a professor of English at the University of Northern Iowa. He read an early version of the paper published in this collection at the October 1984 meeting of the Western Literature Association. He has published a pamphlet on Hamlin Garland in Boise State University's Western Writers Series and a Twayne Series volume on Paul Horgan.

Kenneth Lincoln is a professor with the Native American Studies Center at UCLA. His *Native American Renaissance* was published by the University of California Press in 1983.

Ronald E. McFarland is a professor of English at the University of Idaho. He has published essays on 17th-century and modern poetry and is presently working on a Western Writers Series pamphlet concerning David Wagoner. His first full length collection of poems, *Composting at Forty,* was published in 1984 by Confluence Press.

A. LaVonne Brown Ruoff is a professor of English at the University of Illinois at Chicago. Among her recent credits is a bibliography of

American Indian oral literatures, which appeared in *American Quarterly*, 33 (1981).

Kathleen Sands is an associate professor of English at Arizona State University. She has edited *Autobiography of a Yaqui Poet* (University of Arizona Press, 1980) and, with Gretchen Bataille, *American Indian Women: Telling Their Lives* (University of Nebraska Press, 1984).

Kim Stafford recently completed his doctoral work in English at the University of Oregon and has taught at Idaho State University. He resides in Portland, Oregon and continues to write poems. His most recent collection is *The Granary* (Carnegie-Mellon Press, 1982).

William Thackeray is associate professor at Northern Montana College and a consultant at Fort Belknap College. His field is Indian culture and literature. He has published other articles in *Multiethnic Literature of the United States*.

Dexter Westrum is a doctoral candidate at the University of Minnestoa. His dissertation concerns survival in the works of James Welch, Thomas McGuane, and Edward Abbey. He has an essay on Faulkner forthcoming in the *Arizona Quarterly*.

Peter Wild is a professor of English at the University of Arizona. He has written several monographs for the Western Writers Series: James Welch, Barry Lopez, Clarence King, Enos Mills. He edited *New Poetry of the American West* in 1982 with Frank Graziano, and his own *New and Selected Poems* was published in 1973 by New Rivers Press. He has also written studies of pioneer conservationists in eastern and western America.